T0209940

ACTS OF
MAX

ONE MAN'S
DESCENT
INTO
DEMONIC
DARKNESS
AND HIS
DIVINE
DELIVERANCE

GARRY OLSON

WESTBOW
PRESS®
A DIVISION OF THOMAS NELSON
& ZONDERVAN

WestBow Press books may be ordered through booksellers or by contacting:

WestBow Press
A Division of Thomas Nelson & Zondervan
1663 Liberty Drive
Bloomington, IN 47403
www.westbowpress.com
844-714-3454

ISBN: 979-8-3850-1016-5 (sc)
ISBN: 979-8-3850-1018-9 (hc)
ISBN: 979-8-3850-1017-2 (e)

Library of Congress Control Number: 2023919481

Print information available on the last page.

WestBow Press rev. date: 10/25/2023

Dedication and Acknowledgments

To my dad, Max Olson, you were a most intriguing of characters, to say the least, and I learned to love you deeply.

I want to acknowledge my wife, Mary, who went hesitantly yet lovingly on this journey with me in caring for my dad during the last five years of his life; my sister, Connie, and brother, Larry, with whom I shared my life with our dad on his bizarre journey; and our "little" sisters, Yvonne and Marla, whom we love dearly, and our "little' brother, Jon—may he rest in peace from his troubled life. I also wish to acknowledge my three children, the oldest being my son Darek, who was found faithful and obedient during this trial, and daughters Annika and Ashley, who remain a source of joy in our lives. And I cannot forget to thank Dan Milburn, who also rests peacefully in His arms—an author, friend, and classmate who advised me on my endeavor. Dan said to me after reading my manuscript, "Your dad would be proud!"

Here's to you, Dad. You were quite the character!

Contents

Introduction

A MOST MIRACULOUS SUMMER

We all have a story to tell, and few are as miraculously intriguing as that of Max Olson, my dad. He was an ordinary man in many ways yet so compellingly extraordinary in so many other aspects of his unique persona, always remaining an enigma to me until that most miraculous summer. Why God chose to touch his life as He did leaves humankind at a loss to explain. I lack understanding, but I know that I was chosen to write his story. This is the true story of a lifelong atheist whose "unholy trinity of gods" were his mind, muscle, and money. That was all he needed, so he believed.

"I was quite the character, wasn't I?" Dad asked with a twinkle in his eye and a mischievous smile on his face.

"Yes, Dad, you were quite the character," I replied.

I had just finished telling my dad the story of how he had lost his driving privileges and had his driver's license revoked for life, with the recommendation from the lady at the Department of Motor Vehicles that he "never, ever" be tested again! We both had tears of laughter glistening on our cheeks. Although it wasn't all that funny at the time, when looking back on it I could truly appreciate the humor of it all.

And as for Dad, well, he was hearing the story for the first time, and he too found it quite amusing.

Dad could not remember losing his license; as a matter of fact, he could not remember anything he had done or that had transpired in the last fifteen years. He was a real-life Rip Van Winkle, except the only thing that slept was his mind; he was legally insane for all of those fifteen years. He had no idea what year it was, who was the president, or even why he was living in Oregon and not California, the last place he could remember living. Dad had a lot of catching up to do, and I was relating the story of that day with him at the DMV office and his encounter with the very short and very rotund DMV lady.

I had a lot of stories to share with Dad regarding all of his *acts* over the last fifteen years. He had no knowledge of them. He knew he lived with me but had no recollection as to how all that came to be or even how long he had been living with my wife, Mary, and me. The only memory Dad had of the previous fifteen years was that of my son Darek placing his hands on Dad's head and praying for him at what was to be the start of a most miraculous summer.

No, Dad hadn't been in a coma, but he had been diagnosed as psychotic, a victim of an extremely rare late-life psychotic episode from which, we were told, he would never recover. But I knew it was of a demonic nature. For all of those fifteen years, Dad took prescribed psychotic medication for his condition that enabled him to live a somewhat normal existence.

This is the true story of Max Olson, the lifelong atheist who for sixty-five years lived a very successful and productive life materially, but as a husband and father, maybe not so much. He was very good at everything he loved, and most of what he loved involved the ocean. All who knew him, whether as an accomplished welder who built boats, the amateur scuba diver who earned the coveted Big Fish trophy year after year spearfishing, or an extremely successful commercial fisherman, they all admired him and looked up to him. Even when he was placed in the psychotic ward, the other patients admired and looked up to Dad. He was as always the leader of the pack. But at age sixty-five, Dad entered the twilight zone, the dark world of the insane.

Atheist or not, we all have our gods and serve them, and Max had his. His unholy trinity of money, mind, and muscle—like all false gods—was to eventually fail him and betray him miserably!

After losing his sanity at age sixty-five, voicing the words of demons, and being legally and clinically insane for fifteen years, could such a man experience a miraculous healing from the one and true God, whom he had rejected all his life? Could such a man ever regain the mental intellect to reject the false gods he had served all of his life? Could such a man as this find the even more miraculous spiritual healing that comes with an expression of faith in the true God? Could such a man accept the grace and forgiveness found in the death and resurrection of our Lord and Savior, Jesus Christ?

Dad at twenty-two years old, 1948

This is his story, *The Acts of Max*, from his humble beginning to his very end. But then I am getting ahead of the story of Max Olson.

Chapter 1

THE EARLY YEARS

My father, Max Olson, was born two days before Halloween 1926 in Ogden, Utah. He was the second son of Gilbert and Lola Olson, who were the offspring of some of the original Mormon migrants who first settled in what was to become Salt Lake City with Brigham Young shortly after the martyrdom of Joseph Smith. My grandfather Gilbert was the oldest of seven children, all of whom were orphaned when their father was killed as he was trying to repair the wheel on their wagon; it slipped and rolled backward on him, crushing his chest. Their mother had died a couple of years earlier during the childbirth of their youngest sibling, who was still very young at the time of their father's tragic accident. Grandpa was just seventeen at the time, and he became very angry with his family, the Mormon church, and God when he saw his younger brothers and sisters divided up among his aunts and uncles, many of whom did not even live in Ogden but in the neighboring towns. He couldn't understand why they couldn't all stay together; he, now the man of the family, felt sure he could take care of them.

Angered by the actions of his father's family and the church, the young Gilbert changed the spelling of his name from *Olsen* to *Olson*, as if by his very signature he disowned his family, the church, and God. His brothers and sisters and all our cousins on that side of the family spell their name as *Olsen*. But we are the Olsons!

Grandpa was a muscular young Norwegian who was known for his hard drinkin' and his hard fists in barroom brawls and in the rings of semipro boxing matches. He earned his drinkin' money by crawling into the ring on the weekends, when he wasn't busy bootleggin', as this was the Prohibition era. He told us he could hold his own boxing the locals, but he would get paid to be a punching bag when the pros came to town, providing great entertainment for the locals who were all too happy to pay money to see the young Gilbert get his comeuppance. He could make an easy five bucks by getting into the ring with the pros and getting bested—a couple of day's wages for a young man back then.

But his bootleggin', drinkin', and fightin' did not sit well with the Mormon elders, and he was officially excommunicated from the Church of the Latter-Day Saints. It was shortly after his excommunication that he met and courted Lola Malmstrom, a local farm gal of Swedish heritage, who could "plow the fields with the best of them." And this Scandinavian marriage, both contemptuous and caring, was an unlikely union between two very different people that was to produce two very different sons.

Gilbert and Lola Olson, my grandpa
and grandma, 1940

Max was a couple of years younger than his brother, Alvin, and he was our grandpa's favorite, and Grandpa made no bones about it. He loved telling us grandkids the antics of our dad as a boy. He told us of how, shortly after moving his family to California in the 1930s, he came home from work to find his young son, who was around six years of age, lying unconscious in the front yard. With panic gripping his soul, Grandpa leaped from his truck and raced to his son just as the young boy was beginning to come to.

"What happened, son?" Grandpa questioned his young son with his own heart still pounding wildly in his chest.

"Well, I was at the end of the street, and I bet myself I could race all the way home with my eyes closed," the young Max replied, still groggy from the collision. "But I forgot about the tree in the front yard."

Grandpa told us of how he taught his young sons to box. He said he would have them put on the boxing gloves, and since Alvin was two years older and much bigger than his younger brother, Grandpa would tie one of Alvin's hands behind his back "just to make it fair."

"Your dad would grab his big brother's free hand and pummel away, winning that contest with his older brother." Grandpa would howl with laughter as he retold the story. We could readily see how much he enjoyed regaling us with tales of how our dad, his youngest boy and favorite son, devised with sly cunningness a strategy to defeat his much bigger and stronger older brother.

Grandpa also told us the story, much to Grandma's chagrin, of when he had perhaps had a little too much to drink and saw Grandma bent over chopping wood for the stove while he sat on the porch with their two small boys, who just happened to have their BB gun with them. He said he took careful aim with the BB gun and then had one of his boys pull the trigger, absolving him of all guilt. The BB struck Grandma as she was bent over, presenting them with a somewhat oversized target. He laughed heartily as he told his story, with our grandma glaring at him from across the room, finding no humor in his tale as us three small grandkids tried as best we could to hide our giggles.

One of his stories that offers perhaps the best insight as to why our dad was his favorite begins with the two boys, about seven and nine, being given pocketknives for Christmas. They were very excited about their new possessions—so excited that while Grandpa was at work that day, they proceeded to carve their initials into the railing on the front porch. Of course, it didn't take long for Grandpa to take notice.

He called his boys over and said to them, "Since you boys like carving so much, you can go up into the woods and use those pocketknives to cut yourselves each a nice, long switch, and when you have your switches ready, you can bring them back here to me so I can whip your bottoms with them!"

A short while later, our uncle Alvin came back with a

perfect switch. It was about four feet long and about the size of his thumb at the big end. It was a well-suited instrument to deal out the punishment that Grandpa felt his oldest boy deserved. And he proceeded to not "spare the rod" on him as he used the switch that the boy had so carefully selected, trimmed, and delivered to his dad as he was instructed.

Grandpa continued with his story. "An hour goes by, and no sign of your dad. Then, a couple of hours passed, and I was beginning to worry that your dad had decided to run away! More time passed and it was starting to get dark, and still no sign of your dad!"

Now becoming very worried, Grandpa went to the back porch to see if he could see any sign of the young Max. He peered into the twilight, trying to decide if he should head up into the woods and go looking for his missing son or wait a just a little while longer.

"Just then, I see the shadowy figure of your dad. He was moving very slowly down the hill toward the house, draggin' his switch behind him that he had cut for me to spank him with," Grandpa continued. "He finally made it to where I was waiting. He dropped it at my feet, and turning around and bending over, he proclaimed, 'This is the best one I could find!'

"Well that 'switch' was over twelve feet long and the size of my arm at the large end! All I could do was laugh; he never did get his spanking!" Grandpa laughed heartily, and we could readily tell he enjoyed sharing the memories of his spunky and clever younger boy!

And then there was the time when Dad, as a young teenager, was told he had to go milk the cow. It was Uncle Alvin's turn, but Alvin had a football game at the high school that day. Dad resentfully grabbed the milk pails off the back porch and stormed out of the house to the barn in protest, angry at the unfairness of it all. Grandpa said that, as Dad

Chapter 2

MARRIED TOO YOUNG

Dad's high school graduation, 1944

Max was well liked in his class at Marshfield Senior High School in Coos Bay, Oregon, but unlike his outgoing older brother, he was shy and quiet by nature, and despite his powerful build, he did not get involved in sports or any of the other extracurricular activities except for boxing, where he could let his fists do the talking for him. Even Alvin, who was much taller, wanted no part of Dad in the boxing ring, even with both of his hands free, when they were teenagers in high school.

Our mom, Betty Lou Paul, was very popular and ran with the "in" crowd. She was the quintessential sweater girl of the 1940s, and she set her sights on the older upperclassman, who was a handsome, blond, blue-eyed boy with a muscular build. She acquired the nickname Betty Boop from her classmates, and Dad was nicknamed Lil' Abner, both popular comic strip characters of the day. She chased after him and asked him to be her date at all her friends' parties.

But the world was now at war, and Alvin, being of age, enlisted in the Navy. Dad, still too young, was just seventeen at the time of his brother's enlistment. He snuck off without his parents' consent and lied about his age, and he too enlisted in the Navy to join his brother in the Great Conflict. Grandpa was too old, but he wasn't about to let his two boys go off to war without him, so he also lied about how old he was so he could join them in the Second World War. No birth certificates were required at the time, and if someone said he was of age and had a warm body, no one was going to check the records to prove him wrong. As for Grandma, well, she wasn't too happy about being left home alone to work the farm while her husband and two boys went off to war somewhere in the South Pacific, all in the US Navy with their lives in peril.

Grandma and her sailors (left to right): Uncle Alvin,
Grandma Lola, Grandpa Gilbert, and Dad, 1943

After the war ended, all returned safely home, and Max and Betty Lou picked up where they had left off. She was just eighteen and had just graduated from high school when they were married on June 10, 1948, and Dad was just twenty-two years of age. Three babies came quickly. Connie was born a year later, and a year after that, my identical twin brother, Larry, and I were added to the family.

Four generations (left to right): Grandma
Olson, Great-Grandma Malmstrom, and Mom,
holding Connie, our older sister, 1949

Mom, being only twenty at this time with three babies and a husband to care for, was overwhelmed, but then she started out overwhelmed! Mom shared with us the story of when she got up on the very first day of being a married woman and our dad asked her to fix him some oatmeal for breakfast.

"How do I do that?" she asked him.

"Well, you start by boiling some water," he said.

"How do you boil water?" she asked.

Mom wasn't joking. She had no idea how to boil, broil, or bake anything. She had lived the life of a privileged little girl who was never asked to make her bed, do the laundry, or help clean the house, let alone cook anything. Needless to say, Grandma Olson was not too impressed with the newest member of the family. Dad may have been a man's man, but he was a mama's boy!

Dad was reserved and distant by nature, showing little attention, or affection to his new bride, or even to his children. He was all too happy to stop off for dinner at his mom's house, which was next door to theirs; after all, Mom had not mastered the art of cooking, nor did she ever, if the truth be told. Grandma, on the other hand, was all too willing to continue to take care of her "baby boy," making him both breakfast and dinner every day. Not surprisingly, within a few years the marriage crumbled. Mom packed up and left with her three toddlers in tow, and she began her new life without our dad.

Dad and Mom with us kids, 1950

Olson family, 1951

Mom, like Dad, was unprepared for adulthood and quickly entered into a rebound marriage that lasted only a couple of months. She had the marriage annulled; completely unaware she was pregnant by the man with my baby brother, Jon.

Now, with all hopes of reconciling with Dad gone, she

headed with her four offspring to California to live with her two cousins. An Air Force base was nearby, and the young, attractive single gals had a steady parade of suitors knocking on their door. It was there that she met and fell in love with James "Jim" Everett Wells. James was in the Air Force, and when his enlistment was up, he took Mom and Jon to Illinois to be married by his dad, James Franklin Wells, who was an ordained Baptist preacher. My sister Connie, my twin brother Larry, and I remained in Oregon with Grandpa and Grandma Olson. Dad was living several hundred miles away at this time, and I don't remember him visiting us during those few months.

Mom and Jim came back and got us, and we all headed back to Illinois to be near his relatives, where we welcomed the newest member of our family, my baby sister Yvonne. But jobs were scarce, and after a little more than a year we packed our bags and moved back to Oregon. And surprise—several years later we had another baby sister, Marla. Money was tight for the young family now with six kids, but we were family.

Left to right: The author, Larry, Jon,
and Connie, holding Yvonne, 1958

Chapter 3

THIS IS YOUR "DADDY MAX"

Top Photo:
Us in our Sunday Best 1954
Larry, Connie, and The Author
Bottom Photo:
Inspiration for the Waltons', Maybe? 1955
Larry, Connie, and The Author

Our dad was a dutiful father, if not an affectionate one, to his three offspring, and when we returned to Oregon, he was there to meet us. He had made plans with Mom to get us for the court-ordered visits every other weekend. He arrived with his new wife, Lorraine. I remember Mom telling us that day that "Daddy Max" would be coming to pick us up and take us for the weekend. *What? I thought Jim was our dad,* I remember thinking. After all, that's what we had been told to call him and had for the past year or so. Sure enough, up pulled this car, and a big man and a very petite lady with bleached-blond hair got out of the car. With our hair neatly combed and faces scrubbed, Mom had her three oldest kids lined up to greet them on our front porch.

"Connie, Garry, and Larry, this is your Daddy Max," Mom informed us. Our curious younger siblings peered out the front room window, watching the spectacle unfold before them.

When our parents had divorced, Connie was four, and Larry and I were just three years of age. Connie was now six and Larry and I were five, and I couldn't remember our dad. But, per the divorce agreement, we left for the weekend to spend time with Daddy Max. That first night, we stayed at our grandparents' house, where Larry and I shared a bed with this stranger we were told was our dad. *Connie's lucky,* I thought. *She gets to sleep with Grandma!*

The next morning Dad got up early without waking us. I woke up, and the stranger was gone! Our bed was upstairs in the unfinished attic area, and the walls were lined with rough fir boards. Somehow, I had gotten turned around in the bed during my sleep so that, when I awoke, not only was the stranger gone, but I also could not see the stairway down since I was facing the opposite way. All I could see was a boarded-up wall, and my heart began to race with fear. I thought this stranger had boarded us up in the attic in the middle of the night. In a panic I awoke my brother to let him know of our plight, and it was only then that I saw the stairs at the other end of the room leading down to the main house. Breathing a sigh of relief, we got up and dressed ourselves and then cautiously tiptoed downstairs, hoping to find Grandpa and Grandma. We were relieved to find Grandma at her stove fixing her men breakfast. At least they seemed to know this Daddy Max.

Dad had not improved on his ability to show affection, and the transition to spending every other weekend with these strangers was very difficult for me in the beginning. Lorraine, our new stepmom, helped with the transition process as I found her to be caring and understanding of the trauma we were experiencing. But she was the only one; Dad seemed oblivious. He never missed getting us on our visitation weekends or making his child support payments—ninety dollars a month for the three of us. Even in the '50s and '60s this was a modest amount. But his faithfulness in these meager obligations seemed to be the best he could do to show his affection for his three children.

When Larry and I were about eight years of age, we went to a party at the home of one of Lorraine's family members. We felt left out among these strangers who all seemed to know one another but whom we really did not know at all. Larry and I sat on the couch watching all the relatives visit, laughing and enjoying one another's company. Dad saw us sitting there and came over to us. He sat down between Larry and me, put his arms around us, and announced, "I love my boys!" I was in shock; I had never heard him say he loved us before, and as soon as he got up I went running to Lorraine. I needed to ask her what was up with Dad.

Not knowing exactly what I was referring to, she replied, "Oh, never mind your father. He's drunk!"

I was too young to comprehend the meaning of *drunk*, and I thought, *I hope Dad gets drunk more often!* His words that night were sweet music to my young ears, and oh, how I longed to hear them again. More than fifty years would pass before I would ever hear him utter the words, "I love you."

Even though Dad was a lifelong atheist, he nevertheless saw to it that we went to Sunday school every Sunday that we were with him per Mom's instructions. Dad was always respectful of Mom's wishes and never had a bad word to say about her. When we were home at Mom's we seldom missed Sunday school, as the neighbor lady, Mrs. Buxton, would pick us up and take us to the Baptist church in Coos Bay. Mom soon started going too, while our stepdad, Jim, although a preacher's kid, seldom joined us as he was a dairy hand and the milk cows didn't observe the Sabbath.

So we didn't get a break from Sunday school even when our dad had us. One day we asked Mom when we could make up our own minds as to whether we wanted to go to church or not, and she said that she thought we would be old enough when we entered junior high. It was an easy decision for us; all three of us opted not to go, and our dad was relieved. Like our dad, we grew to become, if not atheists, then agnostics, regarding ourselves wise in worldly things and yet we became foolish in the things of God.

Chapter 4

I DON'T WANT TO
LIVE WITH YOU!

Our stepdad, James Wells, was a hard-working dairyman, and for several years he worked for a large dairy business with several farms, and it was his job to relieve the other dairymen who lived on each farm when they needed vacations and days off. He had just been awarded with a new job that would allow us to live in a home on a dairy farm where he would work as the full time dairyman. The home sat on a small hill above the barn and dairy parlor. We had been there only a couple of weeks when Larry and I turned fourteen. We loved playing in the barn, building forts out of the hay bales, and enjoying our new home with its acres of playgrounds, green pastures, forested hills, and a swimming pond that we were eager to try out as soon as the weather permitted.

School had just gotten out for the summer, and Larry and I were busying ourselves playing in the big barn, making forts and tunnels out of the bales of hay.

"Garry, Larry, you boys get up here right now!" we heard Mom holler from the house. Obediently we left our forts and ran up the hill to the house to see what Mom wanted.

She and our fifteen-year-old sister, Connie, had just gotten into a spat, as moms and teenage daughters often do.

"Your sister just told me that if I were to take you over to your dad's house, he would let you kids live with him," Mom announced to us when we arrived at the house. Turning to us, she demanded, "Will you boys set your sister straight?"

"Oh, he would!" was our matter-of-fact reply, and then we quickly turned to race back down to the barn to our uncompleted forts.

"You kids get in the car now! Your dad doesn't want you living with him!" Larry and I looked at each other in astonishment, and then we shot eye daggers at Connie for getting us into this quandary.

Mom could be highly emotional and would often let her emotions get the best of her. We sat in silence in the back seat of the car, not yet realizing that the next few hours were going to change our young lives forever.

Dad always came and got us, I thought anxiously. *Mom never takes us to Dad's. This isn't even his weekend to have us! He doesn't even know we are coming over. How does Mom even know where Dad lives? She has never been there!*

The thoughts tumbled through my mind as if they were garments in the clothes dryer. My throat was getting dry and tight, and my stomach was churning as Mom raced her three captive passengers to their dad's house. We came to a screeching stop in front of Dad's home, and Mom ordered us out of the car. She was going to prove to us that our dad really did not want us living with him full time. She would humiliate our dad by having him admit as much in front of his children—or so she believed.

Mom pounded on the front door. It was a glass-paned door, and I could see Dad sitting in the corner of the living room reading his newspaper.

"Come in," Dad said without getting up to answer the door.

Although he was undoubtedly surprised at our unannounced and unprecedented arrival, he did not show it. But then Dad seldom showed any emotions.

"Hi, Betty. Hi, kids. What brings you over?" Dad asked nonchalantly.

"These kids just told me that if I brought them over here, you would let them live with you," Mom announced, fully expecting our dad to set the record straight in front of his children.

"Betty, we would love to have the kids live with us, but that would be your decision," Dad replied.

About that time, Lorraine appeared at the door from the kitchen. Since Mom had not gotten the response from Dad she had anticipated, she turned to Lorraine and asked, "Well, what about you? You wouldn't want these kids living with you, would you?"

"Betty, we would both love to have the kids live with us," Lorraine calmly responded. "But as Max said, that is your decision."

Without saying another word, Mom spun on her heels and left abruptly, just as she had arrived, but this time without her offspring. She left her three oldest kids standing bewildered at their dad's front door. We meekly entered Dad's home and sat down on the couch. Not much was said for the next hour and a half as we sat in an awkward silence. Dad continued reading the paper as if nothing unusual had taken place. Lorraine returned to the kitchen and proceeded to prepare a dinner that now had three unexpected guests.

Just before dinner was ready, we heard a car screech to a stop in front of the house. It was Mom. *Good,* I thought. *She has come to her senses and has come back for us!* But she did not come up to the house; she opened the trunk of the car and began throwing out brown paper grocery bags filled with our clothes onto the front yard. Mom was sobbing but never

19

looked toward us, and she sped away as quickly as she had arrived without saying word, not even a goodbye. Feeling abandoned, wounded, and embarrassed, we went out to the front yard to collect our clothes with the neighbors watching the ordeal play out from behind their curtains.

Once we were inside, Lorraine brought out the dinner she had prepared and placed it on our TV trays, but we did not have much of an appetite. After dinner, Dad called us together and informed us that we were to write a two-page essay as to why we wanted to live with him.

What? Are you kidding me, Dad? I thought. *Who does this? I don't want to live with you!*

He sent us to the extra bedroom with paper and pencils and instructions for us not to come out until we were done. I remember turning to my sister, who sat between Larry and me at the small desk in the spare bedroom, and saying, "What am I supposed to write? That I don't want to live with him but I have nowhere else to go?"

We turned and stared at our blank papers and then attempted to complete the task that was illogically demanded of us. We wrote of all of our complaints and problems we had living with our mom— real, imagined, and contrived—trying desperately to fill the two pages with something. When we finished, we announced to Dad that we had done the task he had given us. As he started reading the papers, we could see the look of disgust and anger begin to etch onto his face. He would read the first part of one and, without finishing it, slam it down on the table and go the next essay. He never finished reading any of them; he tossed them back at us and gave us what came to be known as "the look," one that only Dad could give.

"Listen, I told you to write *why* you wanted to live with me, not why you *don't* want to live with your mother," he said with unconcealed anger. "I have no interest whatsoever as to why you don't want to live with your mother!"

But this was our dad; he never wanted to hear us say anything negative concerning our mother, nor did he ever speak negatively of her! The truth was that it was easier for us to say why we didn't like living with Mom than to think of reasons why we would want to live with him. We never did finish the papers that Dad requested of us that fateful day, and he never mentioned them again—all of which was fine with us. We would have been hard pressed to come up with any rational reasons why we wanted to live with him, let alone write a two-page essay on the subject.

Chapter 5

CRIMES AND PUNISHMENT

I can't say I liked my dad very much during my teenage years. I could not understand his cold and distant behavior, his bizarre forms of discipline, or the unfairness he displayed in their execution. Oh, I was thankful that he never spanked us; Dad was a powerfully built man who could put the fear of God in us with just "the look." And if I were to tell the neighborhood kids, "My dad could beat up your dad," they would readily agree. Dad seemed so different in his interactions with my friends, and even with my brother Larry, than in his relationship with me. He told me many years later that he had problems with me because I could always talk to Lorraine, something he had a great deal of difficulty in doing. And it was true: of the three of us, I was the closest to Lorraine. She always had time to talk and was so caring and understanding of what it was like to be a teenager and all the social pressures placed upon us. As for Dad—well, he figured that since he had made it, so could we. Actually, he *almost* made it, as it was to turn out.

"I wish I had a dad like yours," one of my friends said to me.

"No, you don't!" I replied.

They all seemed to admire him, and why wouldn't they? He paid attention to them and actually engaged with them when they came over to visit. My underlying jealousy of my friends and my brother fueled my resentment toward my dad all the more.

His bizarre forms of punishment did little to endear us to him. Dad had given us a couple of general rules that he made clear were never to be violated: 1) If you said you were going to be someplace, be there; and 2) No horseplay or fighting in the house.

One evening around Christmas, Dad and Lorraine headed out to a Christmas party, leaving us kids home alone. Lorraine had just wrapped some gifts, and the leftover empty cardboard tubes were perfect for sword fighting. Connie, Larry, and I chose our weapons and were having a blast with our newfound weapons of war. It was only about ten thirty that night when Dad and Lorraine pulled into the driveway unexpectedly. Larry and I were in full view, busy sword fighting in front of the picture window as the glare of headlights announced their early return. Connie was just out of sight; she appeared safe from the wrath that was to come. Hoping against hope that they somehow didn't see us, we ditched our weapons and quickly headed to the living room, where we sat calmly watching TV when Dad and Lorraine came through the front door.

Dad was expressionless and said nothing, but the look on Lorraine's face let us know we were in trouble. Dad went into the kitchen to put some items away, came back into the front room, and announced, "You know my rule: 'No horseplay in the house.' Connie, you can go in and clean the bathroom. I want it spotless! Garry and Larry, grab your coats and get in the car, now!"

"But I wasn't doing anything," Connie protested, lying to

our dad but knowing that he could not have possibly seen her involvement in our horseplay.

"Makes no difference," Dad countered. "You are the oldest, and you should have stopped your brothers!"

While it was true, she was the oldest, we were much bigger than our older sister, and she couldn't make us do anything at that time. The days when she could boss us around were long gone.

Larry and I grabbed our coats, hastily retreated to the car, and were sitting silently in the front seat of his Volkswagen bus when Dad came out. He said nothing to us as he started the van, and we headed south on Highway 101 toward downtown. The silence was deafening as we drove through Coos Bay toward Bunker Hill on the south end of town. Initially I thought he was going to take us to our grandparents. But my worst fears were being realized as Dad turned on the left-turn signal to take the bridge to Eastside that led up through Coos River to Mom and Jim's house.

He's taking us back to Mom's! I thought fearfully. For the second time in our young lives, we would be left off at one of our parents' homes, unannounced. And this time we would not have our sister with us! Connie had always been the one constant in our lives, and the thought of living without her was painful indeed.

Just as I was imagining the worst-case scenario, Dad pulled into the Pan American Tavern parking lot just before crossing the bridge and came to a stop. We were about six to seven miles from our house on the north end of town. *He's not taking us back to Mom and Jim's after all, but what is he doing?* I thought.

"You boys can get out here," Dad calmly announced. "Since you have so much energy to burn, you can walk home."

The winter night was cold, but dry, and the wind was

blowing briskly as we started our trek home, but I was relieved that we were not going to be dumped off at Mom's.

Meanwhile, Dad returned home to find Connie sitting in the living room. She was wondering where her brothers were but was too afraid to ask when Dad entered the house without us.

"Why aren't you in cleaning the bathroom as you were told?" Dad asked.

"I finished it," she replied.

It was, after all, a small room, and Dad had been gone quite a while. He quickly left the living room and stormed into the bathroom. Upon his return he thrust a toothbrush toward her.

"Here, you can use this," he ordered, handing her the toothbrush. "You will be finished only when your brothers get home, and not before!"

Connie got the worst end of this punishment! I thought later when the three of us were able to reunite and safely share our fates with one another.

Chapter 6

A DAUGHTER'S DESIRE

Connie

Connie, age nine, 1958

Connie was a lovely girl with Dad's blue eyes, blond hair, and dimples. She was the apple of his eye, but even she felt the sting of Dad's detachment.

"I just wanted to get to know my dad," she explained as she shared her experience with me. One day she asked him, "Dad, do you think that we could do something fun together, just the two of us?"

"Well, what would you like to do?" he asked.

"We could go bowling," she suggested, thinking, *"How could he possibly say no?"* We lived only a couple of blocks away from the bowling alley.

"No, that wouldn't be any fun," he replied, thinking only of himself, which seemed to be a pattern with him. Although we did share good times with Dad, they were always at his choosing and not ours.

"We could go to the beach for a walk," she suggested, knowing how much Dad loved the ocean.

"No, that wouldn't be too much fun either," Dad responded, unaware that he had just dashed his little girl's dream to do something special with her dad. After all, she was getting older, and soon another man would become the most important man in her life. Connie left for her room; feeling rejected, and never asked Dad to do something special with her again.

Connie was right—Dad did love the ocean but only if he could be in it or on it. He was an avid salmon fisherman, and in the early '60s the season was long, from late spring till early fall. He would roll us out of bed at 4:30 a.m. on the weekends, both Saturday and Sunday. I was beginning to wish I had not decided to stop going to church. Anything would be better than this! We would head down to the boat basin, have our fill of pancakes and maple syrup at the Basin café, and then go down to the docks where his boat awaited us.

Dad's first fishing boat was the *Ole M.* She was a twenty-eight-foot, double-ended, converted English lifeboat, with a foul-smelling diesel engine in the middle of an oversized cabin. It would bob like a cork in the rough Pacific Ocean. Dad never got seasick, so the rough ocean with its high swells crashing around and over us would never send us home early. After all, we were in a lifeboat! Us kids, on the other hand, ran for the rails and bent over, chumming the fish with our partially digested pancakes and syrup. Not a lot of fun for us!

The only thing that would send us home early would be a heavy fog, and oh, how we little unbelievers prayed for the fog to come in. One such morning our prayers were answered, as suddenly a thick, dense fog quickly descended down and blanketed us. We were about five miles out and with no radar, just a depth finder and compass for Dad to take readings with. Dad pulled out the charts, made his calculations, and headed the boat to the Whistler, the buoy that marked the entrance of the bar that would lead to the Coos Bay Harbor.

We could finally hear the faint bellows of the Whistler off in the distance but could not see it. Visibility was extremely limited; we could scarcely see the bow of the boat. We slowly approached the sound of the buoy, hearing it grow louder and louder, but we were unable to see it until we were almost colliding with the behemoth that was swaying back and forth. Its whistle was now deafening! Dad, no doubt on high alert but emotionless as always, seemed unconcerned as we narrowly missed the buoy. It was so close that we could have reached out and touched it. Dad took another reading and headed us into the dense fog between the unseen rock jetties that separated the ocean from the bay and formed the bar to the harbor, our haven of safety.

As quickly as it had descended, the fog lifted, and we found ourselves in the harbor having passed between the rock jetties without ever seeing them. Had Dad miscalculated in his readings, we would have grounded our boat on the sandy beaches that bordered the rock jetties or even, in a worst-case scenario, struck the rocks that formed the jetty. Such a fate had met countless other boats and ships in their ill-fated attempts to get into the protection of the harbor under similar treacherous conditions.

Connie finally told Dad she did not like to go out fishing, and she was allowed to stay home. But Larry and I, seeking

Dad's elusive approval, continued fishing with him and getting seasick on most of the trips.

On one such morning excursion, as Dad maneuvered the boat between the jetties while heading out across the bar and into the ocean to take us salmon fishing, I was hurriedly racing Larry to get my pole baited and into the water first. I managed to finish first and slid my fishing pole into the pole holder before we had even made it across the bar. Whoever got done first could grab some soda crackers and get the best bunk to ride out the rest of the ordeal. I hurriedly grabbed the crackers to soothe my stomach and made myself as comfortable as possible in the prime bunk position next to that foul-smelling diesel motor.

"Garry!" Dad hollered. "You got a fish on!"

Having just made myself comfortable and not wanting to relinquish my spot to Larry, I hollered back over the drone of the diesel engine, "Someone want to get that for me?"

When we returned to the boat basin and were securing the boat, Dad said to me, "You don't really care too much for fishing, do you?"

"No, Dad, I don't," I bravely replied. In fact, I *did* enjoy it, but not every Saturday and Sunday all summer long regardless of the weather conditions.

From that day forward, I never went out fishing with my dad again. Larry, on the other hand, continued to fish with Dad for the rest of the fishing season. Then he too finally confessed that getting seasick takes all the fun out of fishing and said he also would prefer not to go out anymore. Dad went salmon fishing the next season by himself and shortly thereafter bought his first commercial fishing boat, the *Genevra A.* He would fish commercially on the weekends to supplement his income as a welder at Hillstrom's Shipbuilding Company in Coos Bay. But the fishing wasn't work for him; it was his passion. He loved it and the solitude it provided his soul.

Chapter 7

A FISH STORY

Dad and his trophy lingcod, 1963

Dad's love for the ocean was not limited to salmon fishing; he was an avid scuba diver as well and very good at it. He was the president of the local scuba diving club in Coos Bay and was greatly admired by his fellow divers. He routinely won the Big Fish Trophy, and one year he purposely did not report a forty-pound lingcod he had caught just so someone else could win the trophy for a change.

Scuba diving was a relatively new sport in the '50s, and its popularity was enhanced by the TV show *Sea Hunt* starring Lloyd Bridges (father of actors Beau and Jeff Bridges), as Mike Nelson, and we never missed an episode. Nor did we ever miss *Gunsmoke* starring James Arness as Sheriff Matt Dillon, or *Friday Night at the Fights*, which was a boxing show sponsored by Gillette, "the best a man can get." Dad, like his dad before him, was an excellent amateur boxer both in high school and while in the navy. He earned and was awarded the boxing championship title aboard his navy battleship during WWII. But then, Dad always seemed to be the best at whatever he set out to accomplish. He was a master welder where he worked, and he was the first there to be chosen to learn the newly introduced heliarc welding technique. Boxing, fishing, scuba diving, and welding—Dad loved them all. And he excelled in all of them. He told his sons, "If you like a job, be the best at it; if you don't like a job, don't be good at it and the boss will find something else for you to do!"

Scuba diving was the one thing I loved doing with our dad. It was both exciting and somewhat scary to go into the ocean with our gear on and explore the murky depths, swimming through forests of thirty-foot-tall seaweed swaying eerily in the gloomy tidal currents. Fish were everywhere, and I was always on the lookout for that "big one."

One year when we were older, Dad bought us spear guns for Christmas. Finally, we were old enough to have spear guns and spear our own fish that we could take home to eat. *How fun will that be!* We thought as we held our new Christmas gifts. The day finally arrived when we could take our spear guns out and shoot some of the fish we had seen swimming by us so many times in the past. We went out to the Cribs that weekend, which was the first jetty built years ago to tame the Pacific Ocean as it came into Coos Bay but had long since sunken. It was a fishing haven with places for

31

smaller fish to hide and had an abundant source of plant life and smaller sea creatures for their food. After suiting up and getting ready to enter the water with our spear guns in hand, we turned to Dad with our excitement mounting. "How many fish can we shoot?" we asked in excited anticipation.

"As many as you want," he replied.

Larry and I looked at each other in disbelief. True, there was no limit on black cod and other rockfish as they were in abundance, but we couldn't believe that Dad said we could shoot as many as we wanted. Excitedly we entered the water, big-game hunters on the lookout for our first trophies. We got about ten fish apiece and then started competing to see who could get the biggest. We argued later about who had shot the biggest fish once we had them aboard the boat and in the cooler.

When we arrived home, Dad told us to unload the fish we had shot while he went in the house. He came back with two dull knives and explained that we now had to clean them. Hmmm, that wasn't in our plans. Maybe we should have thought this through a little better! It took us most of the afternoon to clean the fish with our dull knives as we heard our friends playing out on the street in front of our house. Finally, we were done, and we went into the house and told Dad we had finished cleaning the fish.

"Well, follow me then," as he directed us back outside and led us into the garage. "Here, take these," he said as he handed us two shovels.

"You can bury the fish guts in the garden, some at each rosebush," he instructed. "And when you have finished burying the fish guts and heads, let me know."

We dug the holes and buried the fish heads and guts in the rose garden and reported back to Dad that we were finished with the task he had given us.

"Well, now you boys can dig some more holes to bury

the fish filets. We got more fish in the freezer now than we can eat. Next time, don't kill anything you are not prepared to eat," Dad lectured us, and then he turned and walked back into the house. For the second time that day, Larry and I looked at each other in disbelief!

Looking back, I understand why Dad enjoyed the things he did. When he was a young man, it was boxing, it was just he and his opponent, with no one relying on him and he relying on no one. When he was welding, he was cut off from the rest of the world, shielded in isolation behind his welder's helmet; it was just he controlling a puddle of molten steel. Scuba diving was the same, just him and the sound of his air bubbles in an eerie environment of solitude, searching for that big fish that like him was seeking its own isolation in hiding, shut off from the world around him in quiet solitude. And when he was out fishing, miles from any land, it was just him and the sea, just like Hemingway's *The Old Man and the Sea,* Dad's favorite novel. Yes, Dad was a very distant and quiet man, especially when dealing with his unseen demons. No matter where he tried to isolate himself, they were always present, unknown to the rest of us. He was battling an unseen opponent that he could not defeat, one that he would need a rescuer to save him from, the One he denied his entire life. Dad needed the One who would love him before Dad loved Him.

Chapter 8

NO KING SOLOMON

Like most kids, we were given chores to do. Dad would never say to us, "Garry, mow the yard" or "Larry, take out the trash." No, that would be too simple. He always said, "Boys, take out the trash" or "Boys, when I get back, I want the yard mowed." And so it was this one summer day as he left for an errand in town. He said, "Boys, when I get back, I want the yard mowed."

Dad left and I turned to Larry to ask him if he was going to mow the yard.

"Nope," was his reply, not looking up from the TV.

"Oh, yes, you are!" I countered.

Larry had the more laid-back personality of the two of us, and I was always the more serious one. Mom said that, even as a toddler, Larry was always carefree and happy-go-lucky, whereas she described me as having the weight of the world on my shoulders. As we got older Larry, used my personality trait against me. He knew that if Dad asked us to do a chore, he could outlast me in resisting. I did not want to get in trouble, so I usually ended up taking out the trash or mowing the yard. But this time would be different, I decided;

I had mowed the yard the last couple of times, and Larry was going to do it this time.

I stood over Larry as he sat on the couch. When he looked up at me, I stated, "You *are* going to mow the yard this time, or I am going to kick your backside!"

Being identical twins, it was pretty much a dead heat if we got into a fight, so we didn't do it very often. On the rare occasions when we did, the one who was the most motivated usually won the fight. And looking up at me, Larry could tell I was motivated.

"OK, OK," he said grudgingly, and he got up and went outside to mow the yard.

When Dad returned from his errands Larry was just finishing up mowing the second part of our yard on the west side of our house. Dad came into the house to find me sitting on the couch watching TV. He said nothing as he put away some items he had picked up, and then he returned to the living room to sit in his chair and read the newspaper as I continued watching *The Twilight Zone*. Larry came in after putting the lawnmower away and plopped himself on the couch next to me.

"Larry," Dad began abruptly, looking up from his paper, "why don't go downstairs and take your measurements for a new wet suit."

I did not like what I had just heard. Every year Dad would make us new wet suits for us to use on our scuba diving adventures, one of the few things I truly enjoyed doing in the company of my father. As still growing boys we would outgrow our wet suits every year. When we were young, since I was generally the larger of the two of us by a few pounds, Dad would use my measurements because if it fit me, it would fit Larry.

Dad was a man of few words. He said what he meant and meant what he said. And I did not like what he had just said for I dreaded what it meant! I walked over to where Dad was sitting and stood next to his chair. Dad did not look up.

"Dad," I began tentatively, fearing that I already knew what his answer would be, "do you want me to go downstairs and compare my measurements with Larry's?"

"That won't be necessary," Dad replied curtly without looking up at me as he continued reading the paper.

I definitely did not like that answer. I decided to be more direct to end this charade.

"Dad, will I get a wet suit this year?"

"No," he replied, still not looking up at me.

"May I ask why?"

Dad put down the paper and stood up. We were almost the same height these days. Looking me intently in the eyes with that look that only Dad could give, he said, "Well, when I left I said I wanted you boys to mow the yard. When I got back, your brother was outside mowing the yard, and you were in here sitting on your backside watching TV!"

Our yard had two sides, both about the same size. Dad hadn't asked whether I had mowed the east side and Larry mowed the west side. He didn't ask if I had mowed the yard the last time, meaning it was Larry's turn to mow it this time. Dad knew none of that and certainly wasn't giving me the benefit of any doubt.

I appealed my case. "Dad, you always tell us when you want us boys to do a chore, 'Boys, I want the garbage taken out' or 'Boys, I want the grass mowed.' Larry always just sits there. He knows he can outlast me! So I take the garbage out or I mow the yard." I continued with my plea. "I have mowed the yard the last two times! The only reason Larry mowed the yard this time is because I threatened to kick his backside if he didn't!"

Dad's face showed his disapproval of my questioning his

decision and having the gall to make a case against it. His glare burned deeply into my soul.

"I expect more from you than I do from your brother," Dad declared, delivering his decision and finalizing his irrational and irrevocable verdict.

I shot Dad a quick look of disgust as I spun and left the room so I would not have to look at him anymore. He was no King Solomon!

How could he possibly expect more from me? I thought, storming away to seek solitude in my room. True, I was ten minutes older than Larry, but I was hardly an older brother. We were, after all, identical twins—conceived at the same time! Only a handful of our classmates could even tell us apart.

Disgusted and still stinging from the absurdity of his unfair and illogical reasoning, I vowed never to talk to this man again unless I had to. Nor was I to go scuba diving with him and Larry that year, or any year after, ever again.

I would watch them drive away on the weekends to explore the ocean and its excitement together, leaving me home alone with my wounds made raw once again stinging with resentment, bitterly torn open each time they left together to enjoy scuba diving in the Pacific Ocean. I now knew how my uncle Alvin must have felt as his father favored his younger brother. A great divide had formed between my dad and me, a divide that would remain in place for many years.

Chapter 9

OH, I WOULDN'T
DO THAT!

Dad was a pretty smart guy. The trouble was that he thought he was smarter than most everyone else and was quite prideful about it. Because of our contentious relationship and my perception that he favored Larry and treated me unfairly, I was always trying to best him. I viewed it as my great challenge in life. There was definitely a combative strife between us, and it was almost impossible for anyone to get the best of him, let alone his teenage son. But, being young and foolish, I was always willing to try, usually to my own detriment and regret.

One weekend I got a call from Gerald "The Gent" Gentry, one of my best friends, inviting me to an overnight party at his house. His parents were going to be gone for a weekend of fun in Reno, and he and his sister, Sue, began planning a party to capitalize on the opportunity. We were just sophomores in high school, and Sister Sue was only a freshman.

Larry and I had mutual friends, but we rarely went anywhere together on the weekends. I think that, as identical twins, we were always trying to establish our own identities. Our friends knew this about us, so usually one or the other of us was invited, but seldom both of us together, and we were fine with that. And since the Gent and I were close, I got the invite.

The Game Was On

How can I get Dad to say I can go? I thought. Dad would be very suspicious no matter how I broached the subject. I decided that a calm, cool, and collected approach would be my best chance for success. "Dad," I said casually, so as not to raise undue suspicion, "Gerald Gentry asked if I could spend the night at his house this Friday. His parents said he could invite a couple of his friends over to spend the night. You know, like a slumber party. Would it be OK if I went?"

"Sure, I don't see any harm in that," Dad said agreeably.

Dad Was Setting His Trap

Wow, that was easier than I thought it would be! I was already anticipating an evening with no parental supervision, a teenager's dream coming true. I turned to head downstairs to my bedroom to celebrate my victory. But my dream was soon to be suddenly shaken to reality.

"Son," Dad called out to me before I could make it to my room, "you know, come to think of it, I haven't had the opportunity to meet Mrs. Gentry and speak with her, and not that I don't trust you or anything like that, but why don't we go into the kitchen and you can give her a call so I can speak with her? This would be a perfect opportunity for me to introduce myself, seeing how you and Gerald are such good friends." Dad said all this with a slight smirk sliding onto his face, giving me a knowing look.

Game On!

He had not only returned my serve; it was coming back hard and fast. "Sure thing, Dad," I replied, trying to play it cool while the wheels in my head spun. "That would be great. I know she would really like to talk with you too," I added just for good measure. "Now would be an excellent time to try calling Gerald's mom. She should be home from work now. You want me to try calling her?"

Dad stared at me intently with a perplexed look. He hadn't seen that one coming!

Bam! Right Back at You, Dad!

Dad followed me into the kitchen, convinced he had me cornered and no doubt thinking about what kind of bizarre punishment would be suitable for my attempting to deceive him. I smiled confidently at Dad so as not to arouse any more suspicion, and I picked up the receiver of the phone on the kitchen wall and dialed. It was a random number, definitely not Gerald's! An unknown lady answered the phone, and I pressed the receiver tightly to my ear so that Dad could not overhear her side of the conversation.

"Hello," the unknown lady said.

"Hi, Gent! Hey, my dad said I could spend the night at your place this Friday, but he would like to talk to your mom first, to introduce himself. You know, he just wants to make sure she is aware that you have invited a couple of us guys over to hang out and play games," I said, trying to sound as cool and innocent as I could, all the while bathing in guilt and deceit.

"Who is this?" demanded the unknown lady. "I don't know a Gent, and I have no idea who you are and what you are talking about! And you and your friends are definitely not coming over to hang out!"

I listened to her intently, all the while looking Dad directly in the eye.

"Well, what time do you expect your mom to be home then?" I asked the bewildered lady.

"Who is this?" she demanded a second time.

"OK, great! We will give her a call back then. Talk to you later. Bye." I concluded the call, talking over the unknown lady who was still demanding that I tell her who I was and what I was talking about as I hung up the receiver.

"So, Dad, Gerald's mom isn't home right now," I began. "She is working late tonight, and she called and told them she won't be home for another hour and a half or so," I explained. "We can call her back in a couple of hours, and you will be able to speak with her then." I said with all the confidence and coolness of a conman.

Ball Is Back in Your Court, Dad!

Dad peered at me purposely, with the piercing probing of a poker player looking for a tell.

"Well, good, we *will* talk to her then," Dad assured me, letting me know I was not going to be let off the hook. He turned and headed to the couch to take his ritualistic nap before dinner. Just what I had hoped and planned for!

Dad stretched out on the couch and was asleep in no time. I slipped silently back into the kitchen where our phone hung on the wall, and with the TV on as my cover, I called Gent, this time for real. Mrs. Gentry answered the phone, and I asked to speak with Gerald. I told Gent what was going on and said that we were going to call back in a couple of hours or so and he was to make sure to be the one to answer the phone. I would then ask for his mom, and he was to put Sister Sue on the phone to role-play Mrs. Gentry. It all rested on

Sister Sue's successfully deceiving Dad, for she would need to pretend to be their mom. With the carefully crafted con in place, I returned to the living room and waited for Dad to awake from his after-work nap.

What's A-matter, Dad? Am I Hitting Them Too Hard for You?

"Hey, Dad," I said when he awoke, "Mrs. Gentry should be home from work now. Do you want me to try to call her?" I asked with a cocky confidence, convinced that my contrived game plan would succeed.

"Yes, let's give her a call now," Dad said, a little surprised that I would bring it up.

I dialed the phone, and Gent answered as we had planned. "Hi, Gerald, did your mom get home?" I asked with Dad intently studying my every move. "Great, would she have time to speak with my dad now?"

Setting My Own Trap

Gent put Sister Sue on the line, and I greeted her as "Mrs. Gentry," explaining that my dad would like to speak with her to make sure she was aware that I was in fact invited over to spend the night with her knowledge and blessing, and, of course, to introduce himself to her.

"Dad, Mrs. Gentry is on the line and is waiting to speak with you," I said as I handed him the receiver.

"Hello, Mrs. Gentry," Dad said very politely, using his best gentlemanly manners. "This is Max Olson, Garry's dad, and I wanted to introduce myself and say hello before I allowed

Garry to come over to spend the night at your home this weekend."

"Well, hello, Mr. Olson," said the fake Mrs. Gentry. "Such a pleasure to speak with you! I cannot begin to tell you how pleased we are that Gerald has such a wonderful young man like Garry as a friend," Sister Sue said, laying it on as thickly as she could. "Some of Gerald's friends we don't really care much for, but Garry, he is such a polite and nice young man. You must be very pleased to have a son like Garry. He is just the kind of young person we like to see our son having as a friend. And I'm sure you must be very proud of your son, aren't you?" Sister Sue was playing her game pretty cool for a freshman.

"Ye ... yes, I am pr ... pr-proud of him," Dad stammered, almost choking on his words. He was trying so hard to be polite to "Mrs. Gentry."

They chatted a little while longer, Dad remaining clueless that his polite cordiality and best gentlemanly manners were being directed toward a fourteen-year-old girl. They exchanged pleasantries and said their goodbyes, and Dad handed me the phone to hang it up.

Match Point!

"You know, son, I have to admit that there for a while I thought you were trying to pull a fast one on me," Dad confessed.

"Oh, I wouldn't do that, Dad," I said, basking in a rare victory over my rival.

Game Over!

Or so I thought that it was a victory. Although Dad never caught me in my deception, sin and rebellion have their consequences. I had dishonored my father and was haunted by my deception—and all the more so when, as a believer years later, the Holy Spirit chastised me as I read the story of another deceptive twin in Genesis 27.

Jacob, like me, was a twin. Jacob, like me, was not his father's favorite son. Jacob, like me, repeatedly lied to his father to deceive him. And Jacob, like me, was transformed from deceptive selfishness to servanthood by the power of God's redemptive grace and mercy made abundantly available to all in the sacrifice of the Father's "obedient Son", Jesus. I, like all sinners, can only confess my sin and failure as a son and a man, laying it at the foot of the cross.

Chapter 10

I HAVE NO MONEY!

Connie, Larry, and I got jobs as soon as we were old enough. Although Dad made good money in those days for a blue-collar worker, he was extremely tight with his money and no allowances were ever expected or received.

We got only twenty dollars for our school clothes each year, which was a minimal amount even in the '60s, with shirts going for three or four dollars and Converse tennis shoes and Levis costing five dollars each! Because we worked and earned our own money, Dad could no longer claim us on his taxes. So he decided in his "wisdom" that we each owed him the fifty dollars that he would be losing because he no longer could list us as dependents on his tax return. Connie and Larry said nothing in rebuttal and seemingly agreed to Dad's assessment of the damages; I on the other hand challenged him—not that he would allow anyone, let alone me, to win an argument with him. But I oftentimes had trouble remaining silent in the face of his asinine demands of us, so once more I tilted with the windmill that was my dad.

"Dad," I implored, "we are saving you a lot of money by working! We are spending our money on things you no longer have to give us money for, like school lunches and clothes!"

"I told you what I expect," Dad said, effectively ending the debate.

Tax season came and went, and Dad never did ask us to pay him, nor did we offer. I guess he allowed me to win the argument by default without ever admitting he was wrong or, more importantly, that his son was right.

My goal in working was to save enough money to buy myself a cool car, and I would need at least five hundred dollars to do that.

Because I was earning only one dollar an hour, it was going to take me a while working after school and weekends to earn that kind of money. But finally, I had my five hundred, and a man in our neighborhood had a 1960 Bel Air hardtop for sale with a V-8 and a Hurst four-speed shifter on the floor. And he was asking five hundred dollars! It was a cool car that I could take Larry to school in, driving past all of our classmates who still had to ride the school bus.

Dad had given me permission to purchase the car even though I wouldn't be sixteen for a couple more weeks and did not have my driver's license yet. The neighbor man chaperoned me as I drove it home after making my big purchase since I had only a learner's permit at the time. When Dad got home from work, he walked around the car.

"Where are the keys?" Dad asked. "Let's go for a ride."

"Dad, it does not have any gas in it, and I don't have any money left over to buy any," I informed him. "I only have thirteen cents left to my name after paying for the car!"

"Oh, we will have enough gas," he assured me. "Give me the keys and jump in. We will check out this new car of yours!"

I handed Dad the keys to the car and reluctantly got in the passenger seat. Ordinarily I would have wanted to drive and take advantage of my learner's permit, but if we were going to run out of gas I didn't want to be the one driving.

Maybe we will just go around the block and I can use some lawnmower gas to get it to the gas station when I get my license, I silently schemed.

As I got in I nervously glanced at the gas gauge—yep, the needle was touching the "E." But Dad seemed unconcerned as he drove right past the street that would have taken us around the block.

"Dad, I don't have any money for gas," I reminded him. "And the car is running past empty," I added.

He did not respond to my plea, and when we got to Highway 101, he put on the blinker and headed south towards Coos Bay. My heart sank in despair.

"Dad, I don't have any money and the car needs gas!" The urgency in my voice was clearly evident. Dad ignored my plight and continued driving into town. He turned into a gas station, and I reminded him yet again, now in a panic, *"I haven't got any money!"*

"Fill 'er up," Dad told the attendant.

Great, I thought. *Dad is going to turn to me and tell me to pay the man, and I won't have the money and I will have to work here the rest of the night to pay the bill!*

When the attendant approached my car for payment, unbelievably, Dad reached for his wallet, grabbed a five-dollar bill, and handed it to the man. When the attendant left to get Dad his change, Dad turned toward me with "the look."

"I don't want you to ever ask me again to fill your car up with gas," he declared, glaring angrily at me.

I didn't ask you this time, I thought silently while raging with frustrated anger towards him.

When I was older, I began to understand that this was Dad's unconventional way of saying he was proud of me. As tight as he was with his money, it was easier for him to pay the five bucks for the first tank of gas than it was for him to say he was proud of his son.

Chapter 11

EXCUSE ME!
EXCUSE ME!

Although my car was cool, it wasn't one of the elite cars at our high school and would not get me in the running for the Car of the Month, this being my ultimate goal in my young life at that time. One day the following the end of that summer, I was downtown and as I was walking back to my car, I saw an older guy standing next to it and checking it over very carefully. As I drew closer, I recognized him as one of the upperclassmen who had graduated a couple of years ahead of me.

"Is this your car?" he asked.

"Yes, it is," I replied, wondering why he was asking.

"My wife really likes your car, and I have lost my license till 1972," he replied. "She doesn't like driving my car, so I was wondering if you would like to trade."

Wow, till 1972? That is, like, forever, I thought. It was 1967 and I was only seventeen, and back then five years seemed like forever. Looking around I saw nothing that I would want to trade for. "Well, where is your car?" I asked with skepticism.

"Right here in this garage," he said as he pointed to the

auto body shop behind us where he worked. "You want to see it?" he asked, knowing that I did.

"Sure, why not," I said with a shrug, figuring this was going to be a colossal waste of my time.

"Well, here she is," he said as we entered the garage. "What do you think?"

I could not believe my eyes! Sitting in front of me was a metallic green '32 Ford Coupe, with rich pearling, a 350-cubic-inch Olds power plant, and Offenhauser heads, set off by a stainless-steel firewall. She was chopped and channeled with cheater slicks and chrome wheels! He started it up for me, and as the V-8 roared to life, I fell in love.

"I am willing to trade with you, but my dad will have to approve it. It's my car," I assured him after a test drive, "but I will still need to check with my dad."

I hurried home and waited anxiously for Dad to arrive home from work. Although I had paid for the car by myself and had paid for the insurance and all the gas except for that first tank, I knew I better ask Dad first. I had earlier vowed not to speak to Dad unless I had to, and this was a definite "had to!" When he got home, I wanted to catch him before he started that ritual nightly nap before dinner.

"Dad, I would like to trade my car for this other guy's car," I told him.

"What kind of car does he have for a trade?" Dad asked with cynicism.

"A Deuce Coupe," I said, barely able to contain my excitement.

"What?"

"A 1932 Ford Coupe. It is a great car, Dad, and I really want to trade my car for it!"

"I know what a Deuce Coupe is! Why on earth would you want to trade your perfectly good car for an old piece of junk?" he sneered.

49

"It is a beautiful car, Dad," I countered, getting worried he would say no. "We can go look at it now," I pleaded. "You can see for yourself what a great car it is!"

"OK, let's go check out this old piece of junk," he relented.

I drove us down to the auto body shop where the car was being kept. The business was closed when we arrived, but we could see the car through the dirty windowpanes on the shop's garage door. It was dark inside the shop, with only the natural light to see the car. Between the dirty glass and dim evening lighting, I was afraid Dad would not be able to see what a beautiful car it really was.

Dad peered through the dirty window scrutinizing the car. My heart was pounding in anticipation as I awaited his decision.

"Well, if you want to kill yourself, go ahead and trade," he finally answered. "But I don't want to have to pay to bury you. So if you get yourself a ten-thousand-dollar life insurance policy that names me as the beneficiary, you can go ahead and make this dumbass trade."

Wow, Dad, I thought. *I don't mind paying for my own burial, but five hundred dollars would give me a great funeral!* In 1967 you could buy a house for ten thousand dollars, albeit a very small and modest one.

The next day I raced to town and stopped at the first insurance agency I saw. I walked in, and the agent greeted me and asked what he could do for me.

"I need a ten-thousand-dollar life insurance policy that names my dad as the beneficiary!" I announced.

"Well, it certainly won't cost you much," he said with a smile on his face, looking at the ruddy-faced teenager standing before him—undoubtedly the first one to come in and ask to buy a life insurance policy. "You mind telling me why on earth a young man like yourself needs a ten-thousand-dollar life insurance policy?"

When I told him the story, he laughed heartily and was still smiling when he handed me the policy. With the policy in hand, I raced home and presented it to Dad, who just shook his head, not quite believing that I had actually bought the policy he demanded. By the end of the day I had myself a '32 Ford Coupe!

The following day, I drove Larry to school in my new hot rod. Hardly any kids saw us arrive that morning, but by that afternoon when school was out, a throng of kids surrounded my car, all wanting to know whose car it was and enviously waiting to see who it was that owned this object of beauty and power.

"Excuse me, excuse me," I said, pushing my way through the crowd as Larry and I slowly made our way to the hot rod that was commanding so much attention. "I need to get to *my* car!"

"Olson!" I heard someone exclaim. "Is that your car?"

"Yes, it is!" I shouted back proudly, unsure of who had asked.

Beaming with pride and looking out the windshield at all the admiring classmates, I fired the beast up. With the motor rumbling, I slowly began rolling forward, parting the crowd as Moses parted the Red Sea. The next month I received my coveted Car of the Month award, and my car and I were featured in our school paper—my life goal accomplished, and I was only seventeen!

Chapter 12

I SAID SHE WASN'T COMING HOME

The last week of my junior year, which was the last week of Connie's senior year, she got married. I told her she holds the record, as the only girl at Marshfield High School who got married before she graduated who wasn't pregnant or at least thought she was pregnant. So it was that our household was short one woman, with Lorraine being the only one left in a household of men, consisting of Dad, Larry, and me. I thought the world of Lorraine, as she was easy to talk to, always seemed to have time for me, and was actually interested in my life. She was the antithesis of my dad.

When summer was over and Larry and I began our senior year, we got home one Friday night and found that Lorraine wasn't there. When Dad got home, instead of hitting the couch before dinner as was his custom, he went to the stove and started making our favorite meal, wilted spinach— wilted by drizzling bacon pieces and the hot bacon grease with vinegar over the fresh spinach. The house smelled wonderful, and I asked Dad while he was at the stove frying the bacon if Lorraine was working late. He would occasionally make us dinner, but it was usually because Lorraine was out of town with her friend Linda on a shopping spree in Eugene, or she was working late.

"She's not coming home," he said as a matter of fact.

I did not like the way he said it but shrugged it off. "Oh, did she go to Eugene with Linda for the weekend?" I asked, hoping to pry more information from this man of few words.

"I said she wasn't coming home!" he snapped. "What don't you understand about that?"

I didn't answer but left to find Larry and tell him that Lorraine had left and wasn't coming home—ever again.

"Larry," I said when I found him, "Dad said Lorraine isn't coming home."

I shared with him my conversation with Dad, and we both knew Lorraine had left for good. Dad hollered to us that dinner was ready, but neither Larry nor I were very hungry. We sat at the small dining table with Dad and the now very empty chair that Lorraine used to sit in, barely touching our dinner.

"What's the matter with you boys?" Dad asked, emotionless as always. "Aren't you hungry?" He on the other hand scarcely stopped shoveling food in his face.

Oh, I don't know, Dad, I thought, my contempt for this man that I seemed to be cursed with for a father growing even more. *Maybe it was because the only rational adult in this household is gone, and we are stuck with you!*

To me, it was unfathomable. I had never heard them fight, ever, and now she was gone. There had been no hint that anything was amiss that morning when we left for school and nothing to prepare us for the possibility of her leaving. Most difficult of all was that she never even said goodbye. Lorraine's name was never mentioned again in our house, at least while Dad was present.

Christmas that year was lacking and joyless. The house seemed so empty and was devoid of any decorations, as well as the Dean Martin Christmas music on the record player that usually filled our home because Lorraine loved his music so much. Dad never seemed to miss a beat, but then Christmas was just another day off to him.

Spring had just begun when Dad announced that he had quit his job and was going to pursue commercial fishing full time this upcoming season. He would be gone, leaving us boys alone at the house, as he would be fishing down off the California coast.

What? I asked myself. *Did he just say that he is leaving two seventeen-year-old boys, still seniors in high school, by themselves in a three-story house, unsupervised?*

"I have notified the police that you boys will be here alone, so they will be patrolling the house closely," Dad cautioned us.

Really Dad, goodbye!

And within the week, true to his word, Dad had packed his clothes and left. Shortly thereafter he met a lady friend in Northern California and moved in with her. We rarely if ever saw him, which was fine with us.

Well, as to be expected, the Olson house became "party central." This is not a recommended situation for two seventeen-year-old boys who are not even out of high school. Larry would have his party Friday night while I took my girlfriend out, and I would host a party Saturday night while he would take his girlfriend out. Some of our friends attended both parties. And many times, kids we didn't even know or who didn't have friends there would show up uninvited.

One night I left around midnight and did not return until two hours later because I was sure we were going to get busted. Parking was allowed only on our side of the street that ran in front of our house, yet the partygoers were parked on both sides of the street for the entire block. I discovered one of my friends, Tim "The Kid" Sexton, busily lining up cars, parking them neatly on the yard of our neighbors behind our house. They had to have been gone for the weekend and probably wondered what had happened to their front yard when they returned home.

Larry got married shortly after our graduation, a ceremony that Dad did not attend, and then I found myself alone in the three-story house. I had never left home; home had left me! I was the only one left in the now very empty three-story house. I grew tired of the constant parties, but my friends continually came around and I would sometimes just leave the house to them. I knew there had to be more to life than partying, but I had no idea what that could be. The trouble with being lost is that sometimes it takes a while to realize that you are lost.

Dad would occasionally show up unannounced, about every three months or so, but he always came during the day, thank goodness! He told me I could stay there rent-free as long as I was going to school, so I seriously considered becoming a professional student. I paid all the utilities and did not get a stipend to live on from Dad, and with Larry not living there to share the living expenses, my money was stretched thin after college tuition and books. But I was determined to make something of myself even if that meant going hungry. Even as seniors in high school, Larry and I had paid for all our food and utilities once Dad left. If I ran out of money, I didn't eat.

I lived there two more years while attending the local junior college, Southwestern Oregon Community College, and then I moved to Portland to continue my education at Portland State University. Dad sold our home shortly after I left. When I returned to Coos Bay, I shared an apartment with a couple of my friends, Jerry "Jay" Richardson and Tim "The Kid" Sexton, before marrying my high school girlfriend, LeEster. I invited Dad to the wedding; but he failed to show up, but I wasn't surprised seeing as how he had not attended Larry's wedding. Three years later, our son Darek was born, and a daughter, Annika, followed him two years after that. But alas, after more than twenty years, our marriage would dissolve. Shortly thereafter I began a new career and life in Salem, Oregon.

Chapter 13

LARRY'S BIG BONUS

Dad's new boat, the *Connie*, 1970

Dad was very successful in his new career as a commercial fisherman and decided after a few years that he was going to build himself a new, larger fishing vessel, the *Connie,* named in honor of sister and his only daughter. He contracted with his former employer, Hillstrom's Shipbuilding Company, to build him the beautiful fifty-two-foot steel fishing boat with mahogany trim. Dad did all the welding on it during the off-season; after all, he was the best, and it saved him a lot in labor costs in the building of the vessel.

He needed to sell his old boat, the *Genevra A*, so he hired my brother Larry to help him refurbish the old thirty-nine-foot wooden vessel. Dad had taken very good care of the old boat, but it needed some fine-tuning to get it into the top shipshape condition that would get him the premium dollar for it.

Larry shared with me the story of Dad's unusual management style, which clearly illustrates some of Dad's peculiarities. One day Larry was helping Dad replace the heavy twenty-foot fishing poles that were on the old commercial boat. Larry said he was holding the rope that held the poles upright on the side of the vessel taut, while Dad was attempting to tie off the lines on the front of the boat.

"Larry, come up here and give me a hand!" Dad hollered.

"Sure thing," Larry replied, and in his usual laid-back style he let go of the rope before jumping down onto the dock. As Larry walked nonchalantly to the front of the boat, the twenty-foot pole came crashing down onto the dock, narrowly missing him.

He told me that Dad just looked at him in disbelief but never said anything because it was he who had told Larry to come and help him. He had never said anything about first tying off the rope! I guess Dad just thought of it as a matter of spilled milk, and he knew all about spilled milk.

Larry said the actual cleanup of the wooden vessel went well at first, but then Dad—ever critical—began to criticize every little detail and step of Larry's progress. The criticism went on relentlessly, and Larry said he was working as hard as possible nonstop, but to no avail. Dad was under a lot of stress trying to get the boat ready for sale before the fishing season was to begin, and even the favorite son was not exempt from his ever-critical nature. Larry could finally appreciate the position I that I had been in during all of my time living with our dad.

Larry said he finally rebelled. Just to spite Dad, he would goof off every time Dad came around, but as soon as Dad left, Larry would work as hard and meticulously as he could. He would not only do what Dad had instructed him to do but what he thought needed to be done as well. (That's showing him, brother! You were a true rebel!)

Dad continued his critical assessment of Larry's labors right up to a couple of days before the boat was ready to be sold. Larry said he had that old boat in mint condition, and although Dad never once voiced his approval, the criticism slowly subsided and finally ceased altogether.

As potential buyers looked the boat over, they never stopped complimenting Dad on his obvious "pride in ownership" and how good his boat looked. Larry said Dad never once credited him for the boat's appearance, and none of the potential buyers knew how much hard work Larry had put into the vessel getting it ready for sale. They just assumed Dad had always kept his boat looking so fine, and although he did keep it looking good, it had never looked *this* good!

One buyer asked Dad his price, and Dad gave him an inflated price that he never expected to receive but that would give him plenty of negotiating room. The buyer immediately agreed to the price, and Dad was ecstatic. He received several thousands more for the boat than he ever dreamt he would! Even then he never thanked Larry for his part in getting the boat looking better than it ever had and commanding top dollar.

The next day, Dad instructed Larry to accompany him to the bank, and he deposited the check he had received for the boat. Then Dad asked him how much he owed him. Larry stated the agreed-to amount, a little surprised that Dad wouldn't remember; our dad was not one to forget things that involved money.

"OK," Dad said as he began to write Larry a check for his labors.

He handed the check to Larry, and Larry was shocked to see that it was for a thousand dollars more than the agreed-to amount! A thousand dollars was a lot of money in the early '70s (almost eight thousand in 2020 dollars).

When Larry questioned Dad about the amount, he replied, "If you don't think you deserve it, don't take it! If you do, well then, it is yours."

This was our dad. He was unable to tell his son he had done a good job or compliment anyone for that matter. He chose to demonstrate his approval with his money, which he highly valued. Dad found it far easier to let his money do the talking for him.

Chapter 14

WHAT IS WRONG
WITH YOU, SON?

I received a rare long-distance phone call from Dad one day, telling me that Grandpa had suffered a severe stroke and was not doing well. Dad said Grandma had called him informing him of the news and that I should go visit them. It seems that they were at the doctor's office as both of them were getting up in years and were both in poor health—Grandpa from his love of beer and Grandma from her love of cakes and cookies. As they were leaving to go home it started to rain, and Grandpa made a brief run for the car and suffered a devastating stroke. I called Grandma and asked if I could come over and visit, saying that I would also be bringing Larry's daughter, Stacey, who was two and a half years old at the time. Larry was living in Colorado while going to school at that time and did not have the means to get home to visit his grandparents. But Grandma informed me that Grandpa had told her he didn't want anyone coming to visit him, no friends, or family. He did not want anyone to see him in this condition, as he was paralyzed on one side and doing very poorly. I told her I was coming anyway and bringing Stacey with me.

I arrived with Stacey and found Grandpa lying on the couch. He did not smile when he saw me, and I could tell he was upset that his grandson was seeing him like this. I understood and told Stacey to go over and say hi to her great-grandpa. She had her aunt Connie's blond hair and blue eyes, and with our curls she looked like a little Shirley Temple. As she walked over to where Grandpa lying on the couch and unable to move, he broke into a big smile. He was very happy to see her. It was his first smile in over two weeks, and it would be his last. I looked over at Grandma and saw tears streaming down her face; she did love this man with whom she had shared a troubled relationship and two sons, after all. That would be the last time I would see the man I admired most in my life, as he died a couple of days later. When Dad arrived at the funeral home, he was emotionless as always, and both of us, in our very different ways said goodbye to the family patriarch.

Grandma was heartbroken, literally, even though she and Grandpa had showed little if any affection for each other in all the years I had known and loved them both. Grandma was not well, suffering from diabetes and poor circulation in her feet. After discovering gangrene in her right foot just a couple of months after Grandpa's passing, her doctors determined it would have to be removed. They amputated her foot, and a couple of days later, as nurses were attempting to get her upright for the first time since her surgery, my heartbroken grandma's heart gave out. She left this world to join Grandpa once more.

Uncle Alvin brought his family down for Grandma's funeral, and Dad came up from California. We as a family gathered at our grandparents' home, which seemed so different with neither of them there. Uncle Alvin wanted to split up their personal belongings right then, as he did not want to make another trip down to do it. Dad on the other hand did not care.

"You can take home with you anything you want. Just don't take the photo albums as I want to go through all the pictures first," Dad informed his older brother, who had no interest in the old photos.

Uncle Alvin proceeded to take everything of value while Dad sat in Grandma's chair looking through the old photos, caring little that the house was stripped bare. Grandpa and Grandma's silver dollar collection containing over three hundred old coins that was kept in a chest on Grandma's dresser was the first item Uncle Alvin removed from the house. I remember, for perhaps the first time, truly admiring my dad as he was not concerned with things of material value but rather was treasuring the memories of his now-gone parents. But this admiration was to be short-lived.

We left in our separate vehicles as we would all be leaving for our homes after the service. It was agreed we would meet at the funeral home for Grandma's ceremony. I was greeted by the funeral home director upon my arrival and ushered to the private family room. I was the last of the family to arrive. As I entered the family room in the sanctuary, I greeted Uncle Alvin and Aunt Gladys, who were seated in the back row with my cousins, Cynthia and Richard. Dad and Connie were seated in the front row of the small private room, with Connie seated in the outside chair and Dad seated next to her. I knew I did not want to sit next to Dad, but I did join them in the front row, leaving a couple of chairs between Dad and me. My normally quiet and reserved dad greeted me loudly, and then turned around in his chair to talk boisterously with his brother, Alvin and his family. Dad was behaving as if he were the "Master of Ceremonies" at some grand event. He was joking inappropriately and talking incessantly, laughing as he made insensitive jokes despite the somber and subdued family of Uncle Alvin's. I quickly grew disgusted at his behavior and once again embarrassed he was my dad.

The funeral got underway and we observed it from behind the tinted windows in the private family room. As the funeral was ending those who had come to pay their respects rose and were exiting past Grandma's casket. A neighbor lady and dear friend of Grandpa and Grandma's approached the open casket where my Grandma laid in the front of the mortuary chapel, as Bobbie drew near she suddenly broke into sobs as she could now see Grandma in repose. After witnessing her emotional response, I could feel my throat tighten and the tears starting to fill my eyes, while at the same time I was acutely aware that my dad was intently glaring at me. I was feeling irritated by his disapproving stare, and I quickly glanced in his direction. He had turned in his chair so that instead of facing the sanctuary, he was now facing and staring directly at me, leaning in towards me with his hands on his knees, his eyes glaring at me in disapproval. Our eyes met briefly before I quickly looked away with contempt.

"What is wrong with you, son?" Dad asked loudly and disapprovingly when our eyes met.

Oh, I don't know, I thought, refusing to look in his direction or even acknowledge his ludicrously inappropriate comment and behavior. *Maybe it's that the man and woman I loved and admired so much in this world are now both gone, and all I have left of them is you!*

Chapter 15

CASH YOUR CHECK

Grandpa Olson, although an alcoholic, never missed work because of his drinking, and he had a heart as big as all outdoors. He was so loving, caring, and proud of us. He was the type of grandpa every kid should have, in spite of that one shortcoming. He would spend long hours playing cards and board games with us. He would allow us to use his .22-gauge rifle to shoot frogs in his pond, and then Grandma would fry them up for our breakfast. Fried frog legs that we had harvested served with fresh farm eggs—it doesn't get much better than that! And then there were the magic tricks that always amazed us, making him a larger-than-life figure to us. Whether it was the quarter crying or the match jumping, he always enjoyed entertaining his grandkids. When we were older, he taught us how to do those magic tricks that had amazed us when we were younger. He always made time for us, teaching us to drive his '52 Chevy pickup truck in the cow pasture, where we managed to burn the clutch up in it. Grandma was not happy about that! And she scolded him emphatically, but Grandpa just turned and smiled, giving us a wink.

He was a generous and giving man, and he never hesitated

to help out a stranger. He was always bringing people who were down on their luck home with him for dinner and giving them money, much to Grandma's chagrin. One night when we were staying at his house, he brought one such person home with him, and after feeding him, Grandpa went into the bedroom where they kept some cash and gave the man a hundred dollars, serious money in the '60s! Grandma was furious, but Grandpa said the man needed it more than they did.

Since I loved my grandpa so much, I guess I wanted my children, Darek and Annika, to know theirs. I imagine I was hoping the years had mellowed Dad and that he would be a wonderful grandpa for my kids, if never a great dad for me. With this as my goal, I put my past hurts aside and tried to connect with Dad. We would load up the car and travel to his home in Castroville, just outside of Monterey, California, for occasional family vacations. But Dad was not his dad or anything remotely like Grandpa, and my kids really did not know him as a loving grandfather any more than I was able to know him as a loving father. But we had enjoyable visits, and Dad would show us all the sites around Monterey Bay. He and I would play a round of golf at the country club to which he belonged but never really bonding as father and son.

On one such visit Dad and I went down to the boat docks at the Monterey Bay Boat Basin to check on his boat. Dad and his now finished boat, which he had named *Connie*, were well known on the West Coast. Dad was known as one of the top fishermen, commanding respect and admiration from fellow fishermen wherever he went. He told me that he once made ten dollars shy of ten thousand dollars in one day of fishing, an unbelievable amount of money for a day's work back then, reserved only for the top athletes and movie stars. At one time he owned three fishing boats, paying in cash for one just for the moorage slip. There was a waiting list to get a moorage slip, and they were going for about twenty thousand dollars each. He sold the boat for what he had paid for it, keeping the moorage slip for himself. Yes, Dad was one of the best at fishing; just like he was in everything he loved doing.

The other fishermen would follow him out, hoping some of his success would rub off on them, and while he was in the docks other fishermen would follow him around asking him questions. While we were down on the docks that particular day, several fishermen approached Dad and asked about the new rigging system he had developed to keep his lines separated when he had multiple fish on. The fishing lines getting tangled could be a problem when the fish were hitting hard and fast, as tangled lines would slow down the process of getting the fish into the boat. And time was money when the fish were biting. Fishermen want to get their fish off the lines and in the ice hold as quickly as possible so that the lines can get back in the water where more fish are waiting. Just one tangled line could cost a fisherman a lot of money. I waited and watched Dad as he showed them how it worked so they could replicate the system on their vessels. You could tell how much these men admired him as they held onto every word he was saying.

As they left, I said to Dad, "Well, you know what they say: Necessity is the mother of invention."

"That's not true," Dad replied quickly, offering no further explanation.

"Well if necessity is not the mother, then what is?" I asked.

"Laziness is the mother," Dad replied.

Reluctantly, I had to agree; he did have a good point.

For his part, when Dad was in Coos Bay on his fishing trips up our way, he would call, and I would drive out to the docks, pick him up from his boat, and then take him out to the house that I had purchased from him several years earlier. It sat on a beautiful four-acre piece of property that his dad had *given* to him—but he had *sold* it to me! The home was just a shack that he and his dad had built years earlier when Dad had first married our mom. But it had a wonderful building site on it that overlooked the valley. Dad had leveled off the building site when he lived there, always planning to build a nice home on it, but he never did. I had designed a home while I was just a sophomore in high school, and now I was building it ten years later on the same spot where Dad had always planned to build one. Except for the septic system and foundation, I was building the twenty-four-hundred-square-foot home by myself with help from my father-in-law, Norm, who was an electrician, and Connie's husband Terry, who was a plumber. As I gave Dad a tour of our almost-completed home, he offered no compliments or even congratulations, but silently toured the unfinished home with me as the guide. He was taking his time to inspect every detail but remained completely silent, offering neither a compliment, nor a criticism.

After we ate an early dinner, he informed me that I needed to get him back to the boat early, as he needed to stop by the bank that was not too far from where his boat was docked before it closed. So we quickly headed out for the bank, and upon arrival I pulled into the parking lot of the bank to let Dad out. I was planning to wait in the car while he took care of what banking business he needed to do. But he hesitated and turned to get my attention.

"Come on in with me, son. You don't need to wait in the car," Dad instructed.

We went into the bank together, and Dad asked the bank teller for a counter check—this is a check that has no account numbers on it, but a customer could use it to write a check with. Dad proceeded to a small table, and we sat down as he made out the check. As we walked back to the teller, Dad, inexplicitly, handed the check to me; it was for five thousand dollars and was made out in my name. This was the late '70s and that was a lot of money then. It's still a nice sum today.

"Cash your check, son," Dad said, nodding toward the teller.

When she saw the amount of the check, a strange look came upon her face and she informed us that she could not cash the check for me.

"It's good," Dad assured her. "You can call my bank and they will verify that there are plenty of funds to cover it."

"Oh, I am sure it is," she replied. "But it is against bank policy to cash a check of this size, as someone could have money in their account and withdraw it before we could get our funds," she explained. "We can take it for him, and in three days he can get his money when it has cleared."

Dad just looked at the young lady, pondering his next move.

"Well, you will let him open a checking account with it today, won't you?" Dad asked.

"Yes," she replied meekly.

"Son, open a checking account with it," Dad said smugly. Looking the young lady directly in the eyes, he continued, "Then go to your bank, write yourself a check, and deposit it into your checking account, and you will have your money today!"

Dad had both the teller and me speechless. When we returned to the car, I was still numb from what had just taken place. But I remembered to thank Dad, and he said nothing in return. We rode in silence to the dock where his boat was secured; he got out, nodded at me, and then turned and headed down to his boat.

Yes, it was true—as much as Dad loved his money, it was easier for him to part with it than to tell his sons he was proud of them.

Chapter 16

TWIN SALVATION

Meanwhile, after the end of his second marriage, Larry left for Colorado to attend the Colorado Technical College and get a fresh start in life. While there, he was radically saved and left the trade institute for a Nazarene seminary. When he returned home he attempted to share the "Good News" with his twin brother—that what we had been taught in Sunday school as young boys was true!

He shared with me how he trusts in God to provide for him. He told me the story of one day in particular when his faith was amazingly proven to be true. He said he was walking home from the seminary to make himself some lunch when he encountered a homeless man who asked him for his spare change.

"I have no money," Larry answered. "But I am going home to my trailer to make myself lunch. I don't have much, but what I have, I will gladly share with you. My trailer is in the park right over there, just across that walking bridge that crosses the creek."

"What are going to have for your lunch?" the man asked.

"I have a half loaf of bread and a can of corn," Larry

answered. "I was going to make myself a corn sandwich. I will make you one if you if you would like."

"What's a corn sandwich?" the man asked with a puzzled look on his face.

"Well, it is two slices of bread with canned corn for the filling," Larry replied.

"Is that all you got?" the man asked, clearly disappointed and unsure of the proposed sandwich.

"Yes, it is," Larry answered. "But you are welcome to it."

"What are you going to eat for dinner then?" the man asked incredulously.

"Well, to be honest, I don't know, but I trust God to provide for me," Larry declared.

The man, obviously hungry, followed Larry to his trailer. As they crossed the walking bridge Larry looked down to the creek below them and saw a trout floundering in the shallow water. He hurdled over the railing and jumped into the water, where he grabbed the trout. Lifting it over his head, he announced triumphantly, "God has provided! Today, we have trout for lunch!"

The man stood staring in wide-eyed astonishment.

"Hey, guys, you are not going to believe this, but Larry is a Jesus follower," I proclaimed, sharing the startling news with our friends with whom we had partied in high school.

I may have been a little wild growing up, but I had nothing on my brother, and I was having none of this conversion story. I debated the gospel fiercely with him when he returned home. I loved debate and was good at it. When Larry shared his defense of the gospel, I would reply with clever counterarguments. And Larry, being just a new Christian, was woefully unprepared to respond with sound apologetics.

"Just because you are a better debater than I am does not mean you are right," Larry said emphatically in frustration.

The comment would haunt me. At the same time, I had a friend, Andrew, at work who was trying to witness to me.

And what if what we learned in Sunday school as kids was true? For me to be condemned for what I believed was one thing, but it would be another thing altogether if my children followed in my beliefs just as I had followed in my dad's. I certainly wasn't prepared for them to follow me into eternal condemnation!

"The trouble with you Christians is that you are close-minded, you are not open to consider any truth other than your own," I told Andrew.

"Oh, do you have an open mind?" he countered.

"Yes, I do," was my prideful and defiant response.

"Well then, I challenge you to read this book with *your* open mind," he said as he handed me a book that he had brought to work with him that day, hoping that I would accept and read it. It was Josh McDowell's book *Satan Is Alive and Well.*

Full of pride, I accepted his challenge. I took the book home with me just to prove to him that I, unlike Christians, had an open mind. As I read it I found myself laughing and snickering at what I saw as the absurdity of it all, but I would catch myself and get serious, doing the best I could to read it with an open mind. Being as prideful as I was, I was going to prove to him that unbelievers have open minds, unlike Christians. Eventually, the book started making sense—we *do* live in a fallen world and there *is* a battle in the spiritual realm. I began to realize that Satan doesn't care if you don't believe in him; as a matter of fact he prefers that you don't. If you think of Satan as just a cartoonish character in a red suit with horns, a pitchfork, and a pointed tail, perfect! For if you believe that Satan is a mythological cartoon character and is not real, then you will soon believe the same regarding Jesus, God's Son. If there is no Satan, then there is no need for Jesus, the Christ, who came to die for our sins, the sinless One who sacrificed Himself for all sinners. Yes, it all was beginning to make sense to this sinner. He paid the price I could not pay. He was the Lamb of God, the ultimate and final sacrifice who bore the sins of the world as He hung on that wooden cross. We cannot earn our salvation; it is a free gift from God. The Bible says that if you have the Son, you have life; if you do not have the Son, then you do not have life (see 1 John 5:12). I had an existence, but I did not have life. My faith was in myself, and I knew all too well how weak I truly was.

It was during this same time that I would watch Jim and Tammy Faye Bakker on TV in the morning as I drank my coffee, just for laughs. They both seemed to be over-the-top clowns, taking advantage of thousands of good and hapless people. But God uses sinners to do His work, as that is all He has to work with! For we have all have sinned and fall short of God's glory (see Romans 3:23). And God's Word does not return void, no matter whom or what sinner is sharing it, whether they wear no makeup or have it painted on in clownish proportions like Tammy Faye. One morning those overdone red lips said something that I could relate to: "You don't have to change anything to come to the Father; He will accept you just the way you are! He will change the desires of your heart." Tammy seemed to be speaking directly to me through those unseemly, garishly painted lips.

"OK, God," I prayed. "I will seek you with my whole heart, and if your Word is true then I will find you. If your Word is a lie, then I won't find you, and I will have lost nothing. I will change nothing, except that I will seek you with my whole heart. And if I should find you, then your Spirit will change the desires of my heart and I still will have lost nothing but gained everything."

I recalled part of a Bible verse I had memorized in Sunday

school as a six year old, so many years earlier: If you seek, you shall find (see Matt. 7:7b)

God's Word is true! And I found Him waiting for me to return. Just like the father in the parable of the prodigal son, He ran to embrace me, the son who was lost but now is found (see Luke 15:11–32).

And so it was that God put the unlikely trio of Larry, Andrew, and Tammy Faye Bakker together to witness to me, as He left the ninety-nine and sought to find the one that was lost and return me to His flock (see Matthew 18 and Luke 15).

Chapter 17

MAX'S UNHOLY TRINITY FAILS HIM

Larry shared with me the story of his attempt to witness to our dad. He had flown out from the Boston area where he lived to visit Dad, who was showing Larry the beautiful scenery around the Monterey Bay area. At one particularly scenic area where they had stopped, they exited the car to take full advantage of vista before them. Larry thought it the opportune time to subtly witness to Dad: "What a beautiful sight God has created for us to view!" Larry exclaimed.

"What makes you think I believe there is a God?" Dad tersely replied with a look of contempt etched in his face and a demonic glaring in his eyes. Then he declared as he intensified that ungodly glare, "There is no God!" With this one statement, Dad brought about his own demise, descending down through that dark demonic door.

Larry said the look he saw on Dad's face was one of pure evil and demonic in nature, and a chill ran down his spine. Larry related that, in the past, Dad had casually responded that he didn't believe in God, but this time it was different. On this occasion Dad was declaring there was no God; Dad was willfully doing the work of the Enemy! A most dangerous undertaking indeed, as Dad would soon find out.

We all have gods that we serve, and if it isn't the one and true God, we will find another and serve that one. Yes, we all serve our gods, and we all have faith. Dad was no different than the rest of us, and he served his unholy trinity of mind, money, and muscle. His faith was in them and his service was to them.

Like all who are separated from God, it was Dad's pride that anchored that separation, just as our faith in Christ anchors us to God. Yes, we all serve and have faith, but if we do not serve the one true God, and have faith in what Christ has done, then our gods will fail us and our faith in them will not save us. And Dad was to learn this painful lesson.

Shortly after Larry's visit with Dad I received a phone call from our dad, which was most unusual, as back then long-distance phone calls cost money and Dad seldom called me when we lived close to each other, much less when it required a long-distance phone call. That would cost him some of his valued money. I answered his call and concealed my shock. Dad sounded very different that night. Instead of being the reserved man of few words, he was talking a mile a minute. Instead of the cool and composed dad I knew, he was as giddy as a junior high boy.

Dad was in love. He told me he had found the perfect woman, and he was going to ask her to marry him, even though he had only met her three weeks earlier. To say I was in shock is to say the very least; Dad had always told us he would never remarry, and now he was telling me he was going to marry this woman he had only known a few weeks? I feigned excitement for him, wished him well, said goodbye, and then sat down to ponder all of what he had just told me.

About a week later, I was at work in my office in North Bend when I received a phone call from Connie, saying she just got a call from Dad's new fiancée and that we needed to talk right away. She said she wanted to meet in person and asked if she could come to my office.

"Sure, come over now if you would like," I said. I could tell something was very wrong, as Connie would have told me over the phone what was up if it were a simple matter.

Connie arrived, and I ushered her into my office and closed the door. She proceeded to tell me that Dad's new fiancée, Jean, had called her and told her that Dad hadn't bathed or changed his clothes in over a week and was acting very strange.

"Define *strange*," I said.

Connie responded with more of the bizarre news she had heard from Jean, this stranger whom we had yet to meet. "She said that besides not bathing or changing his clothes, Dad was using a lot of curse words and his behavior was erratic with nonstop talking."

"Cursing? Well, that would be strange for Dad, all right," I responded, yet I was still mindful of my recent conversation with him and his uncharacteristic, incessant, and somewhat incoherent rambling about his new "love."

Neither Connie nor I had met Dad's fiancée, and I was wondering what kind of fruitcake he had gotten himself mixed up with who would say such unbelievable things about him. True, Dad had been a sailor and was a fisherman, but I had never heard him use curse words—not because he was trying to be a righteous man, as he was an avowed atheist, but rather because he thought such language was a sign of ignorance and of a limited vocabulary. Dad's not using curse words was merely a manifestation of his perceived superiority over the other sailors and fishermen. And although Dad may not have bathed regularly when he was out fishing in the middle of the ocean by himself with the odor of fish on him, he was meticulous in his grooming when he was in port, always looking sharp and presentable even in casual or work wear.

What on earth is this woman trying to pull, I thought.

"Well, let's try calling Dad now," I said to Connie. "We should be able to get an idea if he is OK if we can talk with him ourselves."

I dialed his number, and surprisingly he answered right away. Even after hearing Connie repeat Jean's story about him, I was not prepared for what I heard coming from his mouth. He was talking in rapid-fire style, and virtually every other word was a curse word. He seemed agitated and wasn't talking in a coherent manner, making no sense at all. Even with the removal of all the vile cursing, he would not have made any sense.

"Who *is* this?" I whispered to Connie as I pointed to the receiver and held it out so that she could hear Dad's expletive-laced tirade.

The look on her face said it all. I cut the conversation short, and we decided that she should fly down to visit Dad and try to figure out what was going on with him. I told her that if she needed any assistance I would fly down and join her. It was the first of the month, and I would be busy getting our merchandisers lined out and informed on how and where store displays would be built. It was a critical time as our monthly sales success depended on getting the month off to a smooth start. I would stay in Oregon, but I told Connie I would be ready to go on a moment's notice if she needed me.

Dad had long before placed everything he owned in his name and Connie's name, and this was fine with Larry and me. Dad's boat, house, stock portfolio, and savings and checking accounts were all in his and Connie's names. From a strictly financial standpoint, it was just as if they were married. He knew that, if anything were to happen to him, Connie would take care of things and fairly split his remaining estate with my brother and me. Knowing this, I told Connie that Dad was to pay for her trip from his checking account as it wasn't like Connie was going down there for a vacation to visit with her dad. She agreed to this, made her flight arrangements, and then asked Dad to meet her at the Monterey airport. And off she went, unsure of what was awaiting her.

I was in bed and sound asleep that night when my phone rang at one in the morning. It was Connie, and she was extremely distraught.

"Dad was arrested and in jail when I arrived at the airport!" she exclaimed. "His fiancée Jean met me, seeing how he was sitting in jail. She drove us straight to the county jail and I posted his bail to get him out, and when I finally got him back to his house he was arrested again! He is currently under a seventy-two-hour psychiatric hold! Something is terribly wrong with our father."

"What?" My mind was reeling. Maybe I was still asleep and this was all a bad dream. Dad had never even so much as received a traffic citation in his entire life, and now Connie was telling me that he has been arrested twice in the same weekend and was being held in a psychiatric ward?

"I need you down here now!" Connie cried out to me. "Today has been a day from the twilight zone. I am beat, mentally, physically, and emotionally, I don't even want talk about it right now! It makes me sick to my stomach, and I am too spent. I will tell you all about it when you get here. I need you down here, now, right now! I just need to find a bed and collapse, if I can sleep after all that has happened since I got here. I have already booked your flight. Be at the Portland airport at 10:00 a.m. tomorrow morning. You need to come down here, now!"

I had never heard my sister talk like this. She was obviously beside herself, but then I suddenly wasn't feeling that well myself; my head was reeling from what I had just heard.

What on earth did Dad do to get arrested, not just once but twice? I wondered. *And he is now being held in a psychiatric ward?* But I didn't prod Connie as I could hear the exhaustion in her voice and spirit. The next morning I went to the airport and flew down to help my sister with our dad, still not fully grasping the utterly bizarre news about him. It was an unusually long and lonely flight to Monterey—at least it felt like it, with all the unanswered questions swirling in my head. I looked around at the other passengers aboard the flight that morning and wondered if any of them had such unbelievable things happening in their lives right now. Probably not!

Connie and Jean were there to greet me at the airport. It was then that Connie started filling me in on her unbelievable ordeal as Jean drove us to the county psychiatric ward where Dad was being held.

Chapter 18

ENTERING THE TWILIGHT ZONE

"Garry, when I landed at the Monterey airport, it was as though I had entered the twilight zone," Connie began, looking shell-shocked from all she had been through in the last forty-eight hours.

Connie went on to explain that Dad was supposed to meet her when she arrived, but instead she was met by a stranger, Jean, Dad's fiancée.

Jean quickly recognized Connie from the pictures that Dad had shown her of his lovely daughter, but Connie had no idea who this stranger was who had approached her at the airport. She was looking around for Dad, wondering where he could be. After Jean briefly greeted her and introduced herself in the airport lobby, Connie was still wondering where her dad was and why he was not there to meet her.

"Where is Dad?" Connie asked the stranger she had just met.

Jean blurted out the unbelievable story. "Your father has been arrested," she told Connie, scarcely believing it herself. "He went to a Honda dealership in Salinas and stole a car!"

As we were to learn later from Dad's friend, John, it

seems that earlier that day Dad and John went to a Honda dealership in Castroville so that Dad could buy a new car, as Dad was convinced that Hondas were the best you could buy. John said that Dad was acting really strangely that morning, somewhat distraught and beside himself, but John felt he needed to help his friend and agreed to accompany him against his better judgment.

"Your father was super-hyper, dirty, unkempt, and using foul language continuously," John told us. He had never seen Dad act, talk, or look like that. He said that Dad looked and smelled like a homeless person, but being a good friend, he decided he would go with Dad. It was a decision he would regret.

They walked into the first Honda dealership that Dad was to visit that day in Castroville, and Dad asked the salesperson to show him a new Honda. Dad was always very frugal and had never bought a new car in his life. He was dirty, but the salespeople were cordial and polite to him until he started cursing at them. John tried to get Dad calm down and then tried to convince him they needed to leave, but Dad wasn't about to budge. He was going to buy himself a new Honda! Soon the sales manager was alerted to the ruckus and came out to try to calm Dad down and end all the commotion he was causing in the showroom. But Dad started cursing at him too, and the sales manager lost his patience with the foul-mouthed customer. In complete frustration he cursed back at Dad and ordered him to leave the showroom or he would call the police. Finally, John got Dad back to the car. At this point he had had enough of Dad's erratic behavior and asked Dad to take him home. He told us he didn't know what was going on with Dad, but he couldn't talk reason into him. He said Dad never stopped cussing and blaming Honda for his ill treatment, and he went on about how that "man from Honda" cursed at him and Honda would pay for that! Dad dropped John off at his home as requested and then proceeded to drive to another Honda dealership in the nearby town of Salinas.

As Jean drove us to the county psychiatric ward so that we could visit with Dad, Connie continued with her story. It seems that Dad, having arrived at the Salinas Honda dealership, was determined to teach Honda a lesson. This is where he stole, or more accurately, "borrowed without authorization" a new Honda and proceeded to burn up the entire front end of the vehicle as he raced it down the freeway at one hundred miles per hour. At the same time, he was applying the brakes. With the accelerator plastered to the floor and the brakes fully depressed at the same time, the heat rose and smoke began to billow!

"How on earth did Dad manage to drive a brand-new car off the lot, and where did he get the keys?" I asked Connie incredulously.

"I don't know," Connie said, as bewildered and puzzled as I was. "But we can ask them that when we get there this afternoon. They want Dad to pay six thousand dollars to repair the car! I told them you were coming down and I wanted you to look at the car first. That seems like an awful lot of money to repair the front brakes. They said they realize that Dad was not mentally stable when this happened and said they would not press charges if Dad made restitution. I told them that we would stop by there this afternoon and pay for the damage Dad had done to the car if you agreed to it and thought it fair and reasonable. That will be our first stop after we visit with Dad."

Connie was right—that did seem like a lot of money for repairs. It was 1988, you could buy the nicest Honda on the lot for less than fourteen thousand dollars, and they were asking almost half that amount to repair the brakes?

We arrived at the Monterey County Behavioral Health

Ward where Dad was being held for a mandatory seventy-two-hour psychiatric hold and were ushered in to visit with him. When we saw him, he seemed very content and pleased with himself, seemingly enjoying his new accommodations. He was convinced that Honda had orchestrated his arrest and was having him incarcerated, but it was OK because he could call Jean without the call costing him anything. If he were home, he reasoned, it would be a long-distance call that he would have to pay for.

Nice trade-off, Dad! At least he's acting normal as far as saving money on long-distance phone calls, I thought.

"And look here," Dad said, holding up the *Wall Street Journal.* "This was waiting for me this morning at the foot of my bed along with clean underwear! I don't know how they get in here, but a clean pair of underwear was there folded neatly at the foot of my bed this morning when I woke up, along with this *Wall Street Journal!*"

He then shifted his conversation and his attention to his bedroom window. "Here, stand on this chair and look out the window, son," Dad insisted, pulling a chair up to the window. "Tell me what you see out there."

The small window in his room was high and without curtains. Standing on my tiptoes, I was just tall enough to look out into the parking lot that was adjacent to his room, so I passed on his offer of the chair, moving it to one side.

"What do you see, son?" Dad asked, wanting to prove his point, whatever that was.

"I see a parking lot full of cars," I replied.

"Yes, but what kind of cars?" Dad asked smugly.

"Just cars, Dad, all different makes and models," I responded. I certainly was not going to say that there were any Hondas in the parking area!

"No, look closely at the cars," he said. "They are all *new* cars! They are all new cars because they are from the Honda

84

dealership! Honda has kidnapped me and has paid these people to keep me in here," Dad contended.

"Dad, people drive new cars. Most people working at hospitals can afford newer cars. It is just the parking lot where the doctors and the nurses park their cars," I replied, futilely trying to talk reason and logic with a man who seemed to have none.

Dad ignored me and dismissed my rationale, and then he moved the chair back to the window. He told Connie and Jean to each stand on the chair, look out the window, and tell him what they saw. Connie went first, dutifully standing on the chair as he insisted, and looked out the window. She reported to Dad what she saw. It was now Jean's turn. I felt sorry for her as she fearfully climbed onto the chair to look out the window and report what she saw. After this exercise that proved nothing to us but everything to him, Dad plopped down on his bed, stretched out to make himself comfortable, and flipped open the newspaper that was provided for him.

"Look here, I have made about two hundred dollars today, just lying here on my bed," Dad said, pointing to the stock market reports. "How much money have you made today, son?"

"I haven't made a dime, Dad. I am down here with Connie looking after you and trying to clean up your mess!"

Dad ignored my caustic comment and continued, "They asked me what newspaper I wanted, and I told them I wanted the *Wall Street Journal*. And this morning, the *Wall Street Journal* was lying here and it cost me nothing," Dad said jubilantly with a look of great satisfaction radiating from his face.

"Oh, you are paying for it," I informed Dad. "Your friends here may not have the money to pay for their accommodations, but you have money Dad, and the county will send *you* a bill. This weekend, after we pay for the car you wrecked and your stay here, it will end up costing you about twenty grand!"

I was hoping that, by talking about that kind of money, I would get Dad's attention. Normally it would, but he was ignoring everything I was telling him and continued to rattle on, focusing instead on how much it was costing *Honda* to keep him there.

Visiting hours were over, and all the detainees lined up alongside Dad to watch us leave. We were the only visitors who had showed up—and as it turned out, we were the only visitors who ever showed up—and they watched us with great curiosity as we walked across the formidable painted white lines on the floor that surrounded the door area. They were not allowed to step over those white lines, and they seemed fascinated by our stepping over them and walking through the doors to freedom. We waved goodbye to Dad as he stood there with his newfound friends, all lined up in a row and waving to us. Dad, as usual, was admired wherever he went. Even in a psych ward, he was the leader of the pack!

Yes, Connie was right: I had just joined her in the twilight zone.

Chapter 19

CHECK, PLEASE!

From the county psych ward, Jean drove us to a car rental center so we could get ourselves a car. We would need it; Dad had left quite a mess in his wake over the previous seventy-two hours. We said goodbye to Jean. It had been a very long three days for her also, as she had witnessed her "Prince Charming" transform into a frog.

We took off in our rented car toward the Salinas Honda, dealership where Dad had "borrowed" the car. Since they had told Connie that they would not press charges against him if Dad paid all of his damages, we wanted to negotiate a deal with them and check this off our list of things that needed to get done while we were there.

Connie had told them earlier that she wanted me to take a look at the vehicle first. "Garry, I have no idea what I am looking at, or even what I would I want to look at," she explained in frustration. "Six thousand seems like a lot of money to fix a car, and I don't want to be taken advantage of. It's Dad's money that I am spending, and I don't want to spend any more of it than I have to." As we pulled into the covered portico of the Honda dealership's service area, the service center manager recognized Connie from her earlier visit and greeted us. He understood that Dad was not in his right mind and was very sympathetic toward us. After introducing himself to me, he began relating to us what had transpired that fateful afternoon:

We had just finished a five-thousand-mile service on a customer's new Honda; it was her first service since buying the car. Our mechanic parked the car here under this portico just outside my office window. He knew the lady was on her way to pick up her car, so he just tossed the keys on the front seat, figuring since I could see it, it would be secure here parked in broad daylight. Apparently, your dad arrived a short time after that and saw the keys lying on the seat, got in, and drove away with her car. No one saw him arrive, nor did anyone see him leave. The lady arrived shortly thereafter to pick up her car, and it was gone! I told her it was just here and perhaps one of our mechanics had taken it for a final test drive. (*Oh, it was being given a final test drive all right, courtesy of Dad.*) We gave her a loaner and began looking for her car. No one knew where it was, and no one here had taken it.

It was then that I decided to call the police. Two officers arrived shortly thereafter, and as the three of us were standing out front, with me trying to explain to them how we just lost a customer's brand-new car off our lot—a car that literally seemed to have had just disappeared into thin air— your dad pulls up in the missing car and parks it back where he found it. Everything that could be smoking from under the front of the car was smoking. Smoke was billowing out from under the hood and from all four corners of the car as the brakes were completely burnt up. I do not know how he even got the car to come to a stop! The wheels were so hot that when he stopped the car, the plastic wheel covers that are bolted on to prevent theft just fell off, all four of them! They had literally melted off of the bolts that held them onto the wheels.

We could hardly believe what we were witnessing. Your dad nonchalantly got out of the smoking car as we were watching him. As he walked right past us, he said hello, smiled, and proceeded to walk toward his car. The officers asked him to stop, which he did, no questions asked, and he was then ordered to put his hands behind his back, to which he also complied. They then approached him and put him in handcuffs, and then they placed him in the back of their squad car.

They returned to me to ask a few more questions, and then they began searching your dad's car. They found the ashtray full of a white powder and believed your dad was drugged out, but they quickly determined it was just baking soda placed there to absorb odors. About that time, your dad, who was seated handcuffed in the back of the patrol car, started trying to kick out the rear passenger side window! One of the officers tapped on the window and told him to stop what he was doing, to put his feet back on the floor, and to

behave himself. Your dad said, "Yes, sir!" and
he quickly obeyed and waited patiently for
them to finish up with me.

Connie and I were stunned, and he didn't fail to take
notice of the looks of disbelief and shock on our faces.

"I suppose you want to check out the car now," he said,
smiling. "Follow me. We have it out back."

We walked out to the back lot, where we found the new
Honda minus its four wheel covers. He unlocked the car and
popped the hood so I could see the damage there. I could
not believe my eyes; every piece of metal under the hood
had the discoloration that comes from excessive heat. Plastic
pieces made to take heat from the motor were melted and
misshapen from the extreme heat that had been generated
by Dad's test drive. All four tires were shot from hard braking
at excessive speeds, and the wheels were discolored, showing
evidence of being exposed to extreme temperatures.

"Write him a check for six thousand," I said as I turned
and looked at my sister, shaking my head in disbelief.

We got the receipt and the assurance that they would
drop all charges against Dad. We returned to our rental car
and drove to Dad's house to spend the night. I was still trying
to wrap my head around everything that was going on.

On the way, Connie began telling me about Dad's second
escapade, which resulted in his second arrest and which,
unfortunately, she got to witness firsthand.

"But wait, there's more," said my exasperated sister.

After I arrived at the Monterey airport, with
no Dad in sight to pick me up, Jean drove me
to the Monterey County Detention Center so
I could post bail for Dad." She took a deep
breath and continued. "I bailed out Dad, and

Jean said she needed a break from him, so she left for home and I got into the car with Dad. He asked me to drive, but since my glasses were in my luggage and I really should use them when I drive, I told Dad he would have to drive us home. As soon as we got on the freeway, Dad hollered something about Honda and that they were chasing us, and he started accelerating. I begged him to slow down, but he kept on accelerating all the more. Eighty miles per hour, then ninety, and soon we were doing over a hundred miles per hour and I believed my life was over! He pointed out that since no one was passing us, this was proof they all must all be from Honda—paid to *follow* him! And as further proof, he pointed out that they were all new cars, so they had to be from the Honda dealership. I frantically told him that no one was going to pass us. "Cars don't pass you when you are going a hundred miles an hour! Please slow down!" I begged him to no avail.

Where is a cop when you need one? I was pleading with Dad to slow up, but he kept on speeding, passing cars left and right, and I knew this would be my last day on earth alive! Trying to think of something to get him to stop racing us down the freeway, I told him that I was starving and we need to stop and get me something to eat. He said, "OK" and took the next exit, and he found us a restaurant. Still shaking, I got out of the car with Dad, telling him I needed to find my glasses so I could read the menu—and I wanted them with me because I would be doing the driving when we got back to the car! As we headed into the restaurant, we saw some workers putting up a new sign outside of the building. Dad stopped and hollered at them, telling them that they couldn't fool him and he knew who they really were. They were from Honda! And if they would come down from their ladders, he would kick both their behinds! They just looked at him like he was out of his mind, which he was, and shook their heads.

I sat us down at the first table we came to, not hungry at all, just glad that we were out of the car and still alive. We ordered our dinner; I picked at mine, and Dad did not even touch his. A large potted plant was sitting next to our table, which seemed to have captured Dad's attention, and Dad then proceeds to tell me that if you stick a fork in a planter like this one, you can come back in five years and the fork will still be there, and sure enough, he reached over and stuck his fork in the planter! And then he tells me that we can come back here in five years and I will see that he was right. Dad was smiling with that smug smile of his the entire time.

Shortly thereafter a young Black family entered the dining area and sat at the table next to ours. The man who appeared to be the father was one of the largest men I have ever seen; he must have been an NFL football player. They ordered their dinner, and as it arrived Dad took notice of the man. With his plate still untouched, Dad turned around and stared intently at the man's muscular back. At first the man ignored Dad. Finally, with his family clearly distracted by Dad's staring, he turned around and asked Dad politely if he could help him.

Dad said, "You think just because I am an old man I can't take you down? I know who you are. You are from Honda, and you are following me!"

The man replied, "I'm sorry, but I don't work for Honda, and I can assure you that I am not following you or even aware of who you are."

While he was talking to Dad, I was trying to mouth my apologies, signaling to him with my hand twirling by my head that Dad was not in his right mind.

The man was so polite, but Dad would not let up. Finally, the man called the waitress over and asked for his check. He and his family exited, leaving their dinner unfinished at the table. Oh, how I wished I could have at least paid their tab for them.

I looked around frantically for our waitress so that I could ask her to bring our check and told Dad I wanted to leave. I was afraid he would just find someone else to accuse of being from Honda and being paid to follow him. When I got our waitress's attention, I said, "Check, please. We need to leave."

Chapter 20

DAD'S RAP SHEET GROWS

Connie continued. "I had my glasses, and there was no way I was going to let Dad drive us anywhere. I was extremely tired and wanted to take us to Dad's house, but Dad insisted that we drive to Uncle Elroy's home."

Uncle Elroy lived about forty-five minutes out of their way; he was our grandpa's baby brother, and he and Dad were very close. Dad wanted to take Connie to visit him as Uncle Elroy and his wife, Billie, had always thought the world of her. They had no biological children of their own but had adopted a boy who never married, and they had no other children or grandchildren of their own. They thought so highly of Connie that, when Aunt Billie passed, Uncle Elroy gave Dad her wedding ring: a beautiful one-carat diamond solitaire. It was supposed to go to Connie, but when Dad proposed to Jean, he gave her the ring.

As they pulled up in front of Uncle Elroy's house, Connie's heart sank. Parked in front of the house was a brand-new Honda, still unlicensed, with the Salinas dealer's placard in the license plate holder. A lady had just exited the car and was walking to the house across the street from Uncle

Elroy's. As Connie brought their car to a stop behind the new car, Dad jumped out and raced up to the new Honda.

"Look at this, Connie!" Dad exclaimed excitedly, waving his arms and pointing out the new vehicle to her. "Honda is trying to tell me how sorry they are, and they have brought me this brand-new Honda to apologize!"

He walked around the new car checking it out excitedly, fully believing that Honda had it delivered to him. Dad then reached for the passenger door to open it for Connie, but it was locked. Undeterred, he then ran around to the driver's door, but it too was locked.

"They forgot to leave me the keys," Dad said, somewhat bewildered.

"Dad, I think this car belongs to the lady who was getting out as we arrived," Connie replied, trying in vain to reason with him.

"No, this new car was left here for me," Dad insisted. "We need to drive to the Honda dealership and let them know that they forgot to leave me the keys! Get back in the car and let's drive to that Honda place and get my keys for my car right now!"

Dad was adamant, and there were no words that would bring reason to his convoluted mind. He had entered into a dark world where no semblance of sense, common or otherwise, existed.

Connie and Dad left without even approaching Uncle Elroy's home, as Dad was no longer interested in visiting him. Dad now had one mission, and that was to get the keys to his new car. Connie had tried to convince him to at least stop in and say hello to Uncle Elroy, but Dad's mind had a singular focus—and that was "Honda." Since Connie was now driving, she was able to convince Dad that the Honda dealership was closed but that she could drive him there in the morning to pick up the "forgotten keys."

It had been a long day and it was getting dark as they pulled up to Dad's home in Castroville.

"Well, will you look at that", Dad exclaimed as they arrived. "My streetlight has been turned off! Do you know how much it would have to have cost Honda to do that? They would have had to pay the power company hundreds of thousands of dollars to shut off only my streetlight!"

"Dad, I think your streetlight is just burnt out! Let's go inside. I am tired," Connie pleaded with her increasingly irrational father.

Finally, after she managed to get him into the house, Dad started talking about Uncle Elroy again while at the same time continuously dialing 9-1-1 to report his "emergency." He told them that Honda had paid the power company to turn off his streetlight and demanded that the police be sent out immediately to get it turned back on, adding in a generous dose of expletives for emphasis.

"Dad, tell me about the stuff you said Uncle Elroy gave you," Connie said, trying to distract him from his repeated, expletive-laced calls to 9-1-1.

Dad left for his bedroom and returned with a small box. "He was a big war hero, you know," Dad said, as he entered the living room where his confused and emotionally exhausted daughter sat. The box he had with him contained Uncle Elroy's war memorabilia.

Dad opened the box and emptied its contents onto the coffee table. There were two souvenir, replica, nonfunctioning pistols with some paperwork and a small velvet case that contained Uncle Elroy's Silver Star medal that he was awarded for his exceptional heroism during WWII.

Uncle Elroy was getting up in years and had given the medal and war memorabilia to Dad along with Aunt Billie's one-carat diamond ring. Connie, anxious to distract Dad from the burnt-out streetlight and his nonstop calls to 9-1-1, asked Dad to tell her how Uncle Elroy came to be awarded such a prestigious medal, although she had heard the story before from our Grandpa Olson.

"Well, Uncle Elroy was serving in Italy during WWII," Dad began. "They were deep into enemy territory, and he got up early one morning and left his encampment to attend to the call of nature. As he lowered his drawers, his white posterior presented itself to the hidden enemy, and his rear came under attack." Dad said as he chuckled softly. "Suddenly he felt a sharp blow to his rear end as it was immediately shot. Wounded and bleeding, with his pants down around his ankles and not knowing where the enemy was, he opened fire, shooting wildly in the direction of the incoming gunfire. His comrades back in camp quickly dove for cover upon hearing the gunfight. To Uncle Elroy's amazement, he saw a white flag waving from the underbrush, and eight Italian soldiers emerged with their hands over the heads. Holding his rifle in one hand and his pants up with the other, he limped, with his bottom bleeding, into his encampment with the eight enemy prisoners! How's that for heroism?" Dad asked Connie, chuckling at the humorous aspect of the tale.

Dad was still unsettled and anxious, and the telling of Uncle Elroy's heroism in single-handedly capturing eight enemy soldiers did little to distract him from his obsession with Honda. He jumped up continuously to look outside while at the same time making repeated, expletive-laced calls to 9-1-1. He had 9-1-1 on speed dial, so it took just one push of a button to get them back on the line. He was also using his newfound, colorful way of talking to communicate with them, and Connie knew it would be just a matter of time before the 9-1-1 operator's patience would grow thin and Dad would draw unwanted attention from law enforcement.

"Look, Connie! Get up and look at this! Do you see what I

see?" Dad exclaimed, peering out his window through parted blinds.

"No, I don't see anything, Dad. What are you talking about?" Connie replied, her exasperation and exhaustion clearly evident in her voice.

"There is a brand-new Bronco parked under that streetlamp! I bet it is from Honda, and they are trying to trick me into thinking they are not spying on me," Dad said as he pulled the curtains to one side so that Connie could get a good look at the new "intruder" in the neighborhood.

Sure enough, there was a brand-new Bronco sitting under the burnt-out streetlight. Dad wasted no time in calling 9-1-1 again, this time to have someone tow away this covert intruder in his neighborhood. The 9-1-1 operator, talking over Dad's expletives, was unable to convince Dad that he needed to stop calling the emergency number, and as soon as the operator hung up on him, he hit his speed dial and got one back on the phone. If you want the police dispatched to your house, keep dialing 9-1-1 and cuss them out. That will usually do it, and it did!

Meanwhile, Jean became very concerned about Connie's well-being as she remembered that Dad had recently purchased a .38-caliber pistol, and she decided she should call the county sheriff's office to express her concerns. They dispatched a county deputy to Dad's home as a precaution, and outside of the house, the deputy was greeted by a city police officer that had been dispatched to stop the harassing calls to 9-1-1. After a brief exchange of information, they cautiously approached the door together and knocked.

Connie and Dad were sitting on the couch, with Connie asking as many questions as she could think of to somehow distract Dad from his obsession with dialing 9-1-1, when they heard the knock on the door. Dad jumped up, and upon seeing the police officers, he opened the door to greet them. Connie said that, at first, Dad was glad to see them and invited them in.

But just as the first officer stepped on the threshold, Dad yelled, "Wait! You can't fool me. I know who you are! You are from Honda! I'm calling 9-1-1." He slammed the door on the officer's foot. There is a good reason the police wear steel-toed boots!

In the police report that I read later, the police noted that they observed pistols on the coffee table and that Dad had raised his phone to strike them with it, and in response the officers tackled Dad and pinned him to the floor.

Connie said that Dad wasn't attempting to strike them; he was merely raising his phone to speed-dial 9-1-1. But t his sudden movement and the presence of the replica souvenir pistols compelled them to act quickly and burst into the house and tackle him. With Dad pinned to the floor, the officers looked up to see an extremely distraught Connie observing the spectacle unfolding before her in horror.

"Please help my dad! I don't know what is wrong with him!" Connie pleaded with the officers. "He is not thinking rationally, and I have just flown in from Oregon to see if I could help him."

One of the officers took Connie into the dining room to talk with her as the other officer stayed in the living room with Dad. Connie began relaying to the officer all that had taken place since she had arrived in California. She then pleaded with him, saying that Dad desperately needed help.

Just then they heard a commotion in the living room. The officer immediately leaped up to assist his partner, with Connie on his heels. In the living room, they discovered Dad flopping on the living room floor and clutching his chest, pulling a "Fred Sanford"!

"Does your dad have a heart condition?" the concerned officer anxiously asked Connie.

"Not that I am aware of," Connie replied, also worried about her father.

Just then Dad smiled and winked as he looked up at Connie and said, "If you pretend you are having a heart attack, they will go easy on you!"

Dad, now a veteran of being arrested, seemed to know all the tricks. And so it was that when I finally arrived to Monterey to assist my sister, I found Dad locked up on a mandatory seventy-two-hour psychiatric hold.

I had been spared the humiliating spectacle, unlike Connie, who had to witness Dad being arrested, handcuffed, placed into a straitjacket, and driven away in the back of a squad car to the county psych ward.

Chapter 21

THE GREAT
PRISON ESCAPE

The next day when visiting hours began at the mental health ward, we were there to see Dad, and as usual we were the only visitors. The staff even greeted us by name. We met up with Dad, who was sitting in the common area visiting with his new friends. They were all listening intently to their new leader as he told them that, when he got out of there, he would make sure that they all would get out. For just like him, they were being held unjustly, and it would be he who would see to it that justice would be done!

This day, Dad was highly agitated, and he was no longer content with his new digs and his "unfair" incarceration. He was growing weary of being confined to the facility and becoming restless. He had met many new friends, and he was convinced that they were all saner than any of the staff, and after observing and engaging with some of them, I was beginning to think he was right! Dad had been told that, if he would agree to meet with the psychiatrist, he would be released to our custody early. Dad adamantly refused, telling them it wasn't him and his new friends who had lost their minds; it was the nurses in the ward who needed treatment!

We tried our best to get Dad to agree to be evaluated, but no deal. Besides, he reminded me once again that he was making around two hundred dollars a day just lying around, as the stock market was doing well then. He was quite pleased with himself and his investments, and this fact seem to placate him.

"How much money did you make today, son?" Dad asked smugly for a second time, as if to prove he was in a superior position to the two of us.

"Not a single penny and you know it," I snapped back impatiently. "Like I told you, Dad, I am down here taking care of you! We could be out playing golf now if you would just say yes to talk with the psychiatrist. Come on, Dad, talk to the doctor so we can go play a round and get you out of here! We can get some fresh air and enjoy ourselves and have a good time for the rest of our visit while we are down here."

Dad loved golf, and it was our ritual to play a round or two when I came down to visit him. But that was not going to happen with this visit; in fact, we would never get an opportunity to play golf together again.

Trying to change the topic, I asked him, "So Dad, when you returned the car to the Honda dealership after burning up the brakes on all four wheels, how did you get the car to come to a stop? The service manager said the brakes were completely gone and there was no way that the car should have been able to stop."

"Oh, those brake were gone," replied Dad, with a pleased look on his face. "No way they were going to stop that car. I used the emergency brake, of course!"

It's funny how the mind works. Dad was unable to comprehend reality but was still able to use his intellect to solve problems intelligently and plan a strategic course of action after taking into consideration all the surrounding and developing circumstances. This was to become evident when we were given notice that visiting hours would be over in ten minutes. Dad then suddenly informed us that he was leaving with us. He had a plan to escape, in spite of the measures put into place to prevent that from happening. As mentioned earlier, no patients were allowed to cross the broad white line surrounding the exit area. Additionally, a white box was painted around the door area where visitors were to wait until a security officer came and unlocked the door for them. Visitors had to be in the box and patients had to be behind the painted line on the floor, or the door would not be opened. But nevertheless, Dad had his plan that he had carefully thought through, and he was convinced it would work.

"Connie, you go first. I will follow you. And Garry, you will take up the rear," Dad said, laying out his escape plan for us. "Trust me, they will open the door, and we can just walk right out of here together, all three of us!"

"Dad, that won't work. They will stop us, and we will be forbidden to come and visit you the next time," I told him, hoping to dissuade him from him absurd plan.

"It will work!" Dad barked. "You just do what I say and keep your mouth shut, and we can walk right out of here, I'm telling you." Obviously growing impatient, Dad glared at me, upset with my lack of confidence in his plan.

"Connie, just get up and walk out now, and I will be right behind you. Son, just follow me. This will work! Let's go!"

And so the plan of a madman was set into motion. Connie and I played along as we were convinced it wouldn't work. Connie got up and started walking by the front desk area that was near the exit. "Good night," she said loudly to the front desk personnel, trying to garner their attention and get them to look up. "We will see you in the morning!" They looked up, smiled, and waved goodbye to us as Connie and

Dad marched across the formidable white line painted across the floor.

"Good night," I repeated to the staff in a loud voice to make sure they looked up again as I followed Dad across the white line. "We are leaving now—*all* of us!" I said loudly. My efforts were in vain. The other patients were standing dutifully behind the white line, wide-eyed and shocked to see one of their own just walk across the line with the staff looking on and saying goodbye to their leader! The security guard smiled broadly at my sister, said good night to her, and opened the door for her to step out, and then to my disbelief he said good night to Dad and held the door open for him. And just like Dad had told us, he walked through the door to freedom—a door that was being held open for him by the security guard!

Jean was seated in the small room outside of the door waiting for us, and when she saw Dad, her face morphed to instant shock and disbelief. As much as I wanted my dad out of this nuthouse, I wanted him to get the help he needed more. I stopped in my tracks well short of the exit, turned, and looked the guard right in his face.

"Come on, son, we need to go," Dad said as he stepped back in next to the guard, waving his arm at me to hurry up and join them.

His plan had worked just like he said it would. Maybe he was right; the staff were more ridiculous than the inmates! I continued to stare at the guard, and finally I asked him, "Are you just going to stand there with the door opened so that Dad can just walk right through it?"

The guard gave me a puzzled look and then turned to look at Dad, who was now back inside, standing next to the guard and waving for me to come and join them. I just stood there looking at the guard. It finally dawned on him what had just taken place—and that he helped facilitate! He yelled for backup and threw Dad into a headlock as the arriving guard twisted Dad's arms behind his back. They were treating Dad like a common criminal, embarrassed that they had just been duped into abetting his escape. I yelled at them to let go of Dad and stop hurting him; after all, it was they who were negligent in allowing him to walk across the white lines and out of the facility, telling him good night in the process and even holding the door open for him!

"Don't leave me in here, son! If you leave me here, you are not my son!" Dad yelled with desperation in his eyes, both pleading with and threatening me as the two guards who had seized him were now roughly dragging him back to his room with all of Dad's newfound friends staring on in fearful amazement.

The words stung as I looked back at Dad through my now tear-filled eyes. "I'm sorry, Dad," I said softly as my words were getting stuck in my tightened throat. "I just want you to get well, Dad. I just want you to get well!"

Never in my life had I felt so low as I turned and walked through the door to where Connie and Jean were waiting. Their eyes were also glistening as we found ourselves unable to help our dad overcome the dark, demonic world into which he had descended.

Chapter 22

I DON'T KNOW WHAT'S HAPPENING TO ME!

The following day Dad finally agreed to visit with the psychiatrist, and the county agreed to release him under advisement that he seeks continued treatment for his condition. After Dad's session and evaluation with the psychiatrist, Connie and I went in to talk with the doctor and hear his conclusions on what was happening.

"I believe your father has suffered from an isolated psychotic episode," he began. "We rarely see this in people of his age. Usually if one can weather the storms of life that happen during their first forty-five years or so, they can weather most of anything else that might follow after that. For some unknown reason your father had this episode happen to him at the age of sixty-five. We just don't usually see this! Have you ever known your father to act strange before?"

"Well, I always thought he acted strange," I told the doctor. "But then, I just figured all teenagers believe their parents act strange. However, I do believe he acted a little more peculiar than most of my friend's parents from time to time."

Connie spoke up. "About six or seven years ago I got a

call from a lady that Dad was dating at the time. She was a registered nurse, and she told me that they had just gotten in a car with another couple after going out for dinner. Dad and she were sitting in the back seat and everyone was chatting and having a good time. She said Dad suddenly started laughing and continued to do so, uncontrollably and for no real reason. When she discovered that he was unable to control himself, she became very worried. She immediately recognized what was happening to him and told the friend who was driving to take them to the hospital.

"They admitted Dad, and he was in there a couple of days," Connie continued. "I asked Dad about it later, and he said that they had diagnosed him as having a minor nervous breakdown caused by stress and physical exhaustion from the extended fishing trip he had just returned from. Dad told me it was like being in a tunnel slowly traveling to a light at the other end that always seemed to be moving farther away as he approached it. Finally, he said he was able to get to the light and out of the darkness, and he felt shaken but relieved. And he was physically fine other than the experience being very unsettling. He told me that he couldn't remember ever being as terrified as he was when he was in that dark, seemingly unending tunnel."

This was the first time I had heard this story in this context. I had previously understood that he was hospitalized briefly for physical exhaustion after his extended fishing excursion, and quite frankly I had forgotten about it.

"Well, they probably are related; it wouldn't surprise me," the doctor reasoned. "It sounds like they could be, but I believe that your father this time is more seriously impaired mentally and psychologically. I guess the best way for me to try to explain what happened to your father is like this: We all go through life experiencing highs and lows," he said, waving his hand up and down to illustrate his narrative. "Your dad started on a high and began going up, and he just kept on going up and up!" He reached his hand up as high as he could to emphasize his point.

"Will he recover and get better?" I asked anxiously.

The doctor placed his hands back on his desk, folded them together, and with a somber look stated, "I believe your father may have approximately a six-month window to recover. If he snaps out of it during that time, then the prognosis for his recovery is relatively good and he stands a good chance of continuing with his life in his normal state of mind. If he doesn't snap out of it in six months, then his chances of recovery diminish significantly and all the more so with each passing month. The sooner we get him in treatment, the better, as his chances for a full recovery become slimmer as each month passes. I would get him into treatment and medicated as soon as possible. The medicine will calm him down so his mind can relax and hopefully recover, and should he not recover, which is a real possibility, the medicine will allow him to live a somewhat normal, functioning life. His prognosis for recovery is not hopeless at this time, but I don't want to give you a false sense of hope either. He has suffered a serious psychotic episode and is currently completely out of touch with any semblance of reality."

Connie and I looked at each other in dismay, but we held onto the slim hope the doctor had provided us as we got up and left to go get Dad and finally take him home. We checked him out of the ward and listened to him go on and on about the lunatics running the place and how he was going to somehow get his new friends out of there as they were all being held unjustly. It was a long drive home. Dad was convinced that his newfound friends whom we had left behind were being held without cause, and the only people needing help were the doctors and nursing staff, and it would now be up to him to rescue them all. Dad was convinced that he was going to figure out a way to rescue his new friends. He had a new mission to accomplish; he just needed to figure out how to do it!

Connie and I were scheduled to fly out in less than twenty-four hours, and we spent our remaining time with Dad trying in vain to get him to leave with us. But he was having none of it, insisting that there was nothing wrong with him and this was all the fault of Honda. We didn't want to leave him alone in California, but there was nothing we could say to him to get him to change his mind. He adamantly refused to leave with us, and we had families and jobs in Oregon that needed our attention. Sadly, we would have to leave as scheduled, praying that Dad could survive being home alone.

Jean drove the four of us to the airport; there was no way we were going to let Dad drive us. We all tried our best to get Dad to join us on the plane for the last time but to no avail.

As we sat in the cramped waiting area of the Monterey airport, waiting for our plane to arrive, I looked up at the two Black gentlemen who had seated themselves across from us. One was about six feet four, young, muscular, and very good looking, and I recalled Connie's story about the large gentleman in the restaurant. I prayed that Dad wouldn't think these two were from Honda! The other gentleman seated directly across from me looked very familiar, and I thought I recognized him. He looked amazingly like my boyhood hero, "Mr. October" himself, Reggie Jackson! But this man was much shorter than I ever imagined a homerun king like Reggie to be. Fortunately, Dad paid them no mind, and he did not jump to the conclusion that they were from Honda and trying to follow him. I could have reached out and touched Reggie and I really wanted to ask him for an autograph, but I was polite and let them talk to each other without a fan's interruption. Reggie noticed me glancing at him, as I was taken aback by how short he was, but I knew it had to be him. Looking back at me, he took the greeting-card-size envelope that he was holding in his hands and casually, but most certainly, deliberately flipped it over so I could read it; it read "Reggie Jackson." Well, at least I would have one pleasant memory of this trip to the twilight zone! But I knew it wasn't over. Dad's nightmare had in fact had just begun.

We said our goodbyes to Dad and Jean and boarded the plane for the flight home. It was late when I finally got home in Coos Bay, and I hit the bed mentally, emotionally, and physically overwhelmed from the unbelievable events and the experience of the past few days. I immediately dropped into a sound sleep and was suddenly jarred from my unconscious slumber at one in the morning, for the second time. The bedroom phone was ringing loudly—*brrringgg, brrringgg!* Fumbling, I clumsily reached for the receiver. It was Dad.

"Son, you need to come get me now!" I could hear the fear and panic in his voice. "I don't know what is happening to me!"

Chapter 23

WHAT DID YOU DO, GO AND SHOOT YOUR EYE OUT?

Mary and I, in front of one of
her prize-winning quilts.

The very next morning Connie and I arranged with Jean to get Dad on the next flight to Portland. This was prior to the TSA airport security regulations, Jean could walk him to his flight and make sure he got on board and we would be able to meet the flight arrivals right at the gate. Connie and I waited at the gate for Dad to disembark. After a short while he emerged from the tunnel. I was shocked when I saw the look on his face. I have never seen such a terrified look on a man's face before, let alone my father's. Dad's face was pale with fear. He was walking very fast and shot through the gate, neither looking to the left or right but with his gaze fixed straight ahead. He didn't spot us, nor did he appear to be looking for us. He obviously did not know where he was going, but he was going there as fast as he could! We could see the fear etched on his face, gripping his tortured soul, and although Connie and I could have reached out and touched him, he remained oblivious to our presence and shot right by us.

"Dad!" I hollered. He turned his head quickly in my direction, and a look of relief briefly replaced the look of terror. He was obviously relieved to see someone he knew. He quickly reached out and grabbed my hand, and he held it so tightly that it was almost painful. He had the look of a frightened child in his eyes. Connie said, "Dad," and his head snapped in her direction. He quickly grabbed her hand with his remaining hand. Squeezing our hands tightly, he once again shot off for an unknown destination, with us trying to keep up with his frenzied pace. We regained control and guided Dad to the baggage claim area to retrieve his bags. He was a lost soul, physically, mentally, and spiritually.

The four-hour drive to Coos Bay was torturous and bizarre, with Dad was glancing about continuously, talking in a panicked, paranoid patter and nonsensical statements, trying to convince us that the state police were looking for him. For me, it was just four hours of torment; for Connie, since she was the only one with a spare bedroom for Dad, it would be a very long six months. It took a full six months before a doctor was able to get a concoction of haloperidol and lithium that would finally enable Dad to function somewhat normally. Until that time finally came, Connie and her husband Terry had to endure the daily and repetitive rants and ravings of a madman. With the advice of Dad's psychiatrist, who saw no hope of a recovery for Dad, we put his home in Castroville and his beloved boat on the market, as it was apparent to all that he would never have the capacity to fish again. His window of opportunity of ever getting out of this dark tunnel of insanity was seemingly shut forever.

With Dad medicated, he, Connie, Terry, and I flew down to Monterey to close on the sale of his home and his boat. We then began the process of moving him and his possessions to the new home we had purchased for him in North Bend. During the move Dad grew increasingly agitated and was obviously irritated that he was paying all the expenses for us to move him back to Oregon. He may have been clinically insane, but with his medication he could think rationally enough to realize that this move would cost him some of his valuable money. Four plane tickets, a rental truck to move his belongings, the meals, motel rooms, and fuel—the expenses were adding up. Dad had money, more than us, so we were not going to pay to move him. After all, we did volunteer our help to get the tedious job done for him and all three of us had to take time off from work without compensation to do so. But Dad was hardly grateful for our assistance in moving him to Oregon. Every time he had to pay for gas, food, or lodging, he would not hide his displeasure from having to part with some of his money.

Connie, Terry, and Dad rode in the rental truck, and I drove Dad's diesel Volkswagen Rabbit back up to Oregon. The truck was gobbling up the gas, and Dad was grumbling every time we stopped to refuel. Finally the fifty-four-mile-per-gallon diesel VW Rabbit needed fuel, but Dad grumbled about that also. It was a foggy and misty day along the Northern California coast, so I turned on the VW's headlights as I followed the truck. We wound our way through the Redwood-forested drive with its heavy coastal mist obscuring what is usually a very scenic coastal area. I followed the truck into a rest area, and as I got out of the car, Dad came storming back to where I had parked, visibly upset.

"Well, I can see *you* are not paying for the fuel!" Dad said, glaring at me. "Don't you know that that a car uses more fuel when you drive with its lights on?"

"Yes, it does, Dad," I responded. "And if it makes you feel better, I will give you a quarter so that I can be safe driving *your* car back home—with the lights on!"

Dad was not pleased with my response. He turned and stomped off in a huff to use the restroom. I turned to Connie and said, "Good thing he didn't know I was also listening to the radio. He would want another quarter for the extra diesel I was wasting on that small pleasure."

Eventually we made it to North Bend and to the little blue house that would become Dad's new home for the next ten years. Dad did pretty well for several years living there under the positive and calming influence of his medications. I had recently moved to Salem to take a new position with the State of Oregon, and Connie would check on Dad at least once a week, filling his pill minder with his medicine. He was very good at taking his medication as scheduled, and there were never any problems in getting him to do so. He would occasionally run to the store in his "new" Honda that he insisted on purchasing after his faithful VW Rabbit gave up the ghost to get his whole milk, which he loved so much. I think it reminded him of his childhood with fresh milk from the family cow. Connie would make sure he was eating well and had groceries stocked in his cupboard.

Meanwhile in Salem, I met my future wife, Mary. She was considerably younger than I, but she had survived a life-threatening cancer that had cost her her left eye. The experience had matured her well beyond her years. She also had lost part of her eye-socket bone during her life-saving operation and could not use a glass eye; as a result she wore an eye patch to cover her missing eye. She was an intelligent, beautiful, and talented young lady, and I was eager to introduce my future wife to my family in Coos Bay. We stopped at Dad's house, as I wanted her to meet him first. I figured that if he didn't scare her away, this upcoming marriage just might work out. I told her about Dad's condition and shared with her that we would find his door unlocked so we would just walk in without knocking. I went on to explain that Dad was hard of hearing and hated wearing his hearing aids, so his TV would be blaring loudly while he slept on the couch. If we were to knock, he would never hear us and we would be left standing outside for who knows how long. Dad's medication had significantly sapped him of his energy, and he spent at least twenty-two hours of each day in bed or lying on his couch. His once-powerful built had dramatically shrunk, and with his strength deteriorated, he was but a shell of his former self these days. Just as I told her, we opened Dad's front door and found him lying on the couch with his TV volume on high, blaring away. He sat up and smiled broadly as we entered, and he muted his ear-jarring TV.

"Hi, son," he said as I entered with Mary.

"Hi, Dad. I would like for you to meet my fiancée, Mary," I said. "Mary, this is my dad, Max."

"Hi, Max. I am glad to meet you," Mary said as she offered her hand. "Garry has told me so much about you."

Dad shook her hand without bothering to stand up, and then, looking up at the young woman standing before him, he said, "What did you do, go and shoot your eye out?"

Mary laughed, somewhat surprised at his comment. "I never heard that one before! Well, Max, I got cancer a couple of years ago, and they had to remove my eye in order to remove the tumor that was growing behind it."

"How'd ya go and get that?" Dad asked.

Chapter 24

IT WILL BE YOURS
THEN, WON'T IT?

Dad continued to live in the small blue house in North Bend for the next ten years, and for the most part he did pretty well. It was heartbreaking to watch this once mentally sharp and physically powerful man slowly deteriorate as his couch took on the permanent profile of his perpetually prone body.

He took a nasty fall one day in which he smashed a lamp and the end table that it sat on next to the misshapen couch. Dad was unhurt, but the same couldn't be said for his furniture. The end table was ruined, and Dad threw it into the trash. The lamp, with its crushed shade and bent shade holder, was still operable, and it now sat on a dining room chair that Dad had moved in from the kitchen table. The chair was now serving the purpose of the end table that used to sit next to the couch. I drove down from Salem to visit and check on him. He was a little bruised, but nothing was hurt except for his pride. As I visited with him, I found the bent lamp with its crushed and leaning shade sitting on the kitchen chair, which was masquerading as an end table, unsettling. Dad, of course, was unfazed by the new decor. The tilting lamp wearing its crumbled shade seemed to emblematically represent Dad's tilted view of the world with his crushed dreams.

"Dad, why don't we run down to the furniture store and pick up a new lamp and end table for you?" I suggested.

"No need for that. This lamp works perfectly fine," Dad said as he reached over to his bent lamp and turned it on for me to see it glowing brightly. "And this chair is perfectly suited to hold it. I didn't use it when it was at the kitchen table anyway, and now I can," he proclaimed as his eyes twinkled, indicating he was quite pleased with himself for his resourcefulness.

At least he can get some enjoyment from his money by not using it, I reasoned.

"Dad, money is a tool," I said, challenging his logic. "Even the best tool in your garage is of no use if you never use it. You still will have plenty of money in savings for any emergency that might arise."

But Dad remained unconvinced. He was content with his busted lamp on its improvised end table that now held a place of prominence in the living room.

It wasn't as if Dad didn't have money. He did, but he had always been extremely tight with it. But that wasn't what worried Connie and me the most about Dad; it was his deteriorating health from lack of exercise. We informed him that we had found a Nordic Track treadmill that was nonmotorized so he could exercise on it at his own pace. And since it was nonmotorized, it would stop when he did. Additionally it would travel at whatever pace he walked, it was a perfect piece of exercise equipment for him. Dad, of course, did not want to spend the money, but Connie bought it for him anyway on the off chance he would use it. Before he had become ill, he was an avid health enthusiast and would lecture us kids about exercising, eating too much salt, and even enjoying a glass of wine with dinner. Nowadays his interest in any form of healthy living was long gone, and lying around all day suited him just fine. Perhaps the Nordic Track in his front room would motivate him, so Connie ordered it for him. When it arrived, Dad seemed surprisingly pleased. He got on it to try it out and smiled broadly as he showed off for us.

On my next trip down to visit, I asked him if he was getting any more exercise since he had the Nordic Track.

"Oh, I am getting a *lot* more exercise with it in here now," Dad said proudly.

"Good," I said. "I am glad to hear that."

"Yes, I used to be able to walk straight to the kitchen to get something to eat; now I need to walk *all-l-l-l-l* the way around that thing to get into the kitchen," he said, beaming broadly with his blue eyes twinkling and circling his arm to emphasize his point.

If anything was improving with Dad, it was his sense of humor. I don't recall Dad ever having a good sense of humor prior to his illness. But sadly that is the only improvement we saw.

Since his health and mental capabilities were declining at a precipitous rate, we thought it would be good if he would take an Alaskan cruise while he was still able to enjoy life and had the energy for such a trip. Connie approached Dad with the idea. She had contacted his now ex-fiancée Jean and asked her if she would like to take an all-expense-paid vacation with Dad on an Alaskan cruise, if we could get him to agree. After all, she had been very gracious by returning the one-carat diamond engagement ring to Connie after it became apparent to all that Dad did not and most likely would not ever have the mental stability to enter into a marriage. There was no way Dad could go on the trip unsupervised, but he could go with Jean and there would not be any real trouble or problems for her with Dad medicated daily. He could lounge on the deck all day enjoying the sights, and he would definitely enjoy the fine dining. Connie described to him how wonderful it would be and how much he would enjoy being on the ocean, and of course there was the added bonus of getting to see Jean and enjoy her company once again. Dad would have none of it. He was not interested in spending any of his money on such a wasteful endeavor.

He had worked hard all his life, and if he was going to enjoy any of the fruits of his labor, he had to do it soon as his physical and mental abilities were rapidly diminishing. It was now or never! I, like Connie, wanted Dad to enjoy some of his hard-earned money, and a trip on his beloved Pacific Ocean seemed like the perfect opportunity for him to do so. So when I went down to visit him, I decided I would take a more creative approach to convince him to enjoy his life and spend a little of his money on an Alaskan cruise.

"Dad, you have worked hard and have done very well for yourself," I began. "But you won't live forever, and like all of us one of these days you will die. And if you don't spend your money and enjoy it, you will leave it all to us kids. And even though you have done quite well for yourself, if you don't spend any of it, we will! My share will be a nice chunk of money, and I will spend it all in first month, two at the most! "I declared, confident that he wouldn't want that to happen.

Dad looked at me intently. "Well, it will be yours then, won't it?" he replied while smiling up at me, his blue eyes twinkling, completely unmoved by my proclamation that I would someday blow his beloved hard-earned money on wasteful and lavish living.

Chapter 25

I DON'T NEED NO
BLINKIN' LIGHTS!

Dad continued on his mental and physical decline, so I wasn't too surprised when Connie called me and said that he had gotten into a minor accident with another driver. It was Dad's fault, as had he failed to yield the right away to an oncoming car at a stop light, turning right in front of the approaching vehicle. The police officer that arrived at the scene interviewed Dad and determined that perhaps it was time he surrendered his license. So he ordered him to take a license examination to determine his fitness to drive.

Connie had a vacation planned, so she asked if I could come down and escort Dad to the Department of Motor Vehicles office for his court-ordered driver's examination appointment. I told her it would be no problem, and on the day of the appointment, I left Salem early and headed down to North Bend to take Dad to the DMV office in Coos Bay.

I arrived early and helped Dad make himself presentable, and then we went into his garage to get in his car. He wanted me to drive, but I told him maybe he could use the practice. It had been a while since I had ridden with him, and I wanted to see for myself just how alert he was behind the wheel. We started off pretty good, and Dad was traveling a respectable forty-five or fifty miles per hour down Highway 101 as we headed into Coos Bay.

"Holy cow, Dad! You might want to slow up a little!" I exclaimed in an elevated tone of borderline panic, as Dad was failing to slow down upon entering town. But we continued at the forty-five-plus speed as we sped through downtown Coos Bay, failing to slow down even a little.

"The driving instructors put a lot of stock into not speeding when you are taking a driving exam, Dad," I said. "You are doing forty-five in a twenty-five-mile-per-hour zone! Slow down! Now!"

My concern only grew. "What the heck was that, Dad? You just changed lanes without signaling or checking to see if anyone was behind us! And slow down, would you? You might want to look in your rearview mirror, just for giggles. They like to see you doing that!"

Dad paid me little attention, slowing down only slightly as we continued to race through the downtown area. I was shaking my head and thanking God no one was in Dad's blind spot as he just jerked his car over without so much as a glance to see if anyone was in the lane, never mind warning them by using his turn signals. One good thing about his speeding was that no one was going to be sneaking up behind us!

By the grace of God, we made it to the DMV's parking lot without incident, and I had determined that if the DMV didn't pull his license, I was going to. We walked up the steps to the DMV office and notified them that we were there for Dad's appointment, and then we took our seats in the waiting area as we waited for our appointed time to arrive. It wasn't long before a lady came out to get us. She was about four feet nothing and about as big around as she was tall. She escorted us into her office, and after we exchanged introductions and pleasantries, she turned to Dad.

"Max, I am going to ask you a couple of questions just to see how you are doing this morning. First question: Max, can you tell me what day of the week today is?" she asked. Dad, of course, was clueless. I tried to cover for him by explaining that he had been retired for some time and really had no need to track the days of the week closely.

"Very well then, can you tell me what month it is?" she continued.

Dad shook his head and replied, "No." I decided to remain silent this time.

"Well, Max, can you tell me what season it is?"

Dad thought about it for quite a while, and then he leaned to one side to look out the window behind her to get a clue. He answered hesitantly, "Spring?"

Yea, Dad, we got one! I thought.

"Very good, Max. How about the year? Do you know what year it is?" the DMV lady asked.

Dad responded quickly, "1985," with a triumphant sense of confidence.

The only trouble was that it was 1999!

"Not quite," she replied, relatively unfazed by his answer. She allowed only the faintest trace of a smile to sneak onto her lips.

"Let's try something different. Can you spell the word *world* backward for me?"

I could tell the wheels in Dad's head were spinning as I silently spelled it in my head backward, just to make sure *I* could do it.

A big grin appeared on Dad's face. He leaned in toward the DMV lady and asked, "You got a newspaper?"

The local paper was named *The World*, and DMV lady was now unable to hide her smile.

"Okay, let's see if you can briefly tell me something about the following presidents of the United States," DMV lady announced. "Let's start with Harry S. Truman. Can you tell me anything about him?"

"Bombs a lot!" Dad quickly replied. DMV lady briefly pondered his answer and then nodded her approval.

"Dwight D. Eisenhower?"

"Salutes a lot," Dad replied, quite pleased with himself.

"John F. Kennedy?" DMV lady asked, smiling slightly at Dad's last answer.

"Got shot a lot!" Dad replied to the slightly stunned DMV lady.

"Richard M. Nixon?"

"Lied a lot!"

"Gerald Ford?" DMV lady continued, not concealing the fact that she was intrigued and amused by Dad's responses.

"Falls down a lot!"

"Jimmy Carter?"

"Smiles a lot!"

"Ronald Regan?"

"Acts a lot!" Dad replied smiling, obviously delighted with his string of correct answers.

"Whatever you do, don't ask him about Bill Clinton," I interjected, thinking she might not like Dad's answer to that one!

"Yes, it is a good time to stop," she replied, smiling. "Let's see how you do with traffic sign recognition." She pulled out a piece of paper that had the silhouettes of about ten traffic signs on it.

Dad managed to get only one right, the stop sign—two if you count his response to the railroad-crossing silhouette, which he identified as "a railroad stop sign." That too elicited a small smile from the DMV lady, who was struggling at times to maintain her composure.

So I was quite taken aback and surprised when she announced it was now time to take the driving exam. I would have bet money that the exam would never get that far. We left her office, and as we entered the waiting area, I took a seat.

"Come on, son!" Dad hollered when he noticed me beginning to sit down.

"No," DMV lady said. "Just you and me on this one."

Perfect, I thought. I had already ridden with Dad once that day, and I was in no hurry to do it again!

As Dad and DMV lady headed down the stairs to the parking area, I quickly moved to the row of chairs in front of the large windows that overlooked the parking lot. I definitely did not want to miss the show. Smart money was on them not even making it out of the parking lot.

Dad and DMV lady finally entered his car, with Dad getting into the driver's side after DMV lady pointed him to that side. When he approached the car, he apparently had wanted her to drive as he went to the passenger side and opened that door to get in. They sat in the car for the longest time, and I was thinking, *If only I could only be a mouse listening in on their conversation.* It had to be a good one. Dad finally exited the vehicle and opened the door behind the driver's seat, obviously looking for something inside on the floorboards. DMV lady exited the vehicle and watched Dad in disbelief, and she was clearly not happy. Her hands were on her portly hips, and she had a glare on her face as she watched Dad with disgust, her anger obviously mounting. Dad, unable to find what he was looking for in the back seat, then got on all fours and began looking under the car! I was hoping he was going to be able to get up by himself without my having to run down there to help him back to his feet. He finally managed to get his feet under him and stood back up, and the DMV lady's displeasure continued to mount. Dad

125

then opened the trunk lid and began checking inside the trunk. *What could he possibly be looking for?* I wondered. DMV lady said something, and Dad closed the trunk lid. Glaring at him, she briskly signaled for him to follow her back up the steps to the DMV office. Dad's head was drooped and his shoulders stooped, and like a whipped puppy he followed the short, rotund DMV lady back up the stairs and into the building. I quickly returned to my original seat and grabbed a magazine, acting nonchalant as a very upset DMV lady entered the waiting area with Dad in tow.

"Come on!" she barked, waving her short and ample arm at me. "In my office!"

I followed Dad into her office, and she slammed the door behind us.

"How long have you owned that car, Mr. Olson?" DMV lady barked angrily at Dad. Apparently they were no longer on a first-name basis.

Dad was clueless; he had owned it for about two and a half years. He had been insistent on buying himself a new Honda after moving to North Bend when his faithful diesel Rabbit finally petered out. Connie and I were thinking at the time, "Not another Honda!" But with his medication and Connie at his side, he was able to purchase the Honda with no problems.

"He's had it about two and a half years," I answered for Dad. He was standing next to the DMV lady with his head bowed, looking at the floor and surely feeling somewhat embarrassed and humiliated.

"You'd think a man who has owned a car for two and a half years would know where to find the turn signals," she railed.

Dad just stood there with his head hanging down, not looking up at his accuser.

She continued. "He not only does not where to find the

turn signals, he has no idea even where to begin to look for them! He was looking in the back seat and the trunk trying to find them, for crying out loud!" exclaimed the exasperated DMV lady.

Dad finally lifted his head up and pulled himself erect to his full height. Now towering over the DMV lady, he defiantly folded his arms across his chest, looked down at her, and announced, "I do not need to know where those blinking lights are!"

"And why don't you need to know where those 'blinking lights' are?" DMV lady demanded in a demeaning manner while glaring up at Dad with her clenched fists on her full-figured hips.

"Because I don't drive at night!" Dad responded triumphantly. Once again quite pleased with himself, he completely believed he had won this debate.

That's my dad. Just when all hope appears to be gone, he pulls one out of his hat, I thought sarcastically.

"Mr. Olson, I am not only not going to return your driving privileges to you, I am recommending that you *never, ever,* be tested again for a driver's license," she angrily announced as she pointed to the door. "You may leave now!"

As we walked across the waiting area, Dad turned to me. "She seemed a little upset," he remarked, substantially understating the situation.

"Yeah, she did," I replied. "Hand me the keys, Dad. I'm driving."

Chapter 26

NOT ANOTHER HONDA!

Since Dad could no longer drive, Connie and I made the decision to sell his car. Dad did not want to sell it, convinced that he would get another driver's license and get to drive again. He also believed that I had reported him to the DMV and suggested that he shouldn't be driving, and he was for a while very upset that I would betray him and do such a thing. Either Connie was able to convince him I had nothing to do with it or he forgot about it, but it wasn't long before he was no longer angry and resentful toward me. With Dad unable to drive and the car sold, this only added to Connie's responsibilities in her ongoing care for our dad. She would now have to stop by his place almost daily to have lunch with him and make sure he had all the groceries and anything else he might need. It was on one such visit that Dad asked her if she wanted to see his new car.

"What are you talking about, Dad? We sold your Honda," a confused and concerned Connie inquired.

Dad, beaming with pride, took Connie out to the garage to show her what he had just purchased. Sure enough, there was a brand-new Honda sitting in Dad's garage!

My office phone rang. It was Connie.

"Dad just bought himself *another* brand-new Honda," she blurted out.

"What!" I exclaimed.

How was that even possible? Sure, Dad probably had enough money in his checking account to pay cash for a new Honda, but even I was aware that you need a valid driver's license to purchase a car from a licensed dealership.

"Don't worry, Connie," I assured my sister. "I will get Dad's money back. That dealership surely knew that they could not legally sell Dad a car."

Odd as it was, Dad was more than willing to spend thousands of his dollars to purchase a new Honda but was unwilling to spend a small fraction of that amount to purchase a new lamp or end table. Dad's fascination with Honda seemed insatiable.

My phone negotiation with the Honda dealership was very brief. I asked to speak to the sales manager. I told him who I was and informed him that his dealership had illegally sold my dad a car and that I would be down there the following week to return it. I told him I would expect them to have a check ready when I delivered the car to them. He did not argue. He knew full well that Dad was not mentally capable of legally making a purchase of that magnitude, as one did not need a degree in psychology to discern that Dad did not have all his faculties about him. Not to mention that he was an unlicensed driver, and they had allowed him to drive a car off their lot without proof of a license or insurance. I believe that they were expecting that they might get a call and gave me no argument.

When I went down and returned Dad's new Honda, Connie and I both knew that the time had come for us to sit down and discuss Dad's moving in with me. He had a great deal of trouble bathing, as he said the water in his shower was either too hot or too cold. He no longer had the mental acuity to adjust the water valve correctly. In addition, he was becoming more physically unstable, and there was an increasing chance of him falling; he had already fallen once. If he were to fall again, it could be a couple of days before Connie might discover him. It would have been unfair to ask her and Terry to take care of Dad's personal hygiene, and Larry was living on the East Coast near Boston, so he was not considered a viable candidate to care for our dad. Connie expressed her concern that Dad would not get along with me if we had to share a home since we never seemed to get along the last time I lived with him. I, on the other hand, was unconcerned, as Dad had always maintained that people are to follow the rules of the person who owns the house they are in.

"As long as Dad understands it is my home and he is living with me, there won't be any problems," I assured her. "He will follow my rules, as it will be my house."

And so it was that the least-favored son was to be the caregiver of his father in his waning years. We agreed that we would put Dad's house and mine up for sale as my current home really did not have space for Dad and was a split-level house with all the bedrooms located downstairs. Dad would not be able to negotiate stairs on a daily basis, and the coming years would only intensify that problem. Both houses were eventually sold, and I purchased a home in Southeast Salem that would work for Dad, Mary, and our daughter Ashley, who was now in junior high school. As for Dad, he was quite content to move to Salem to live with us, even following the rules of my house because he enjoyed the company and having all his dinners prepared for him.

Chapter 27

IT WON'T HURT
TO TRY

Anyone who has done it can tell you that caring for an aging parent is not easy, and Dad's psychotic condition did not help matters, but then aging brings its own problems regardless of the various accompanying conditions. Dad's psychotic medication worked fairly well, but his psychosis did intensify with each passing year. He would hear his mother calling him and would go outside on the patio to look for her. I told him that occasionally I, too, would dream about Grandpa and Grandma and was always glad when I did. One day he was convinced that his mother was still alive and was calling him, and he did not want to come in the house so he could continue to look for her outside. I went outside and told him that it is wonderful to remember Grandma and have dreams about her, but if she were still alive, she would be over a hundred years old. I reminded him that she had passed years ago.

"Well, that's what that tell me, but I don't believe it," Dad replied.

And then there was his obsession with wanting to go to Astoria to get his boat, the *Connie*, which we had sold years earlier in California. One day while I was at work, I got a call from the Marion County Sheriff's Office. They had found Dad walking down the road about a mile from our house. I started wondering if I would have to move Dad to a home where he would have more supervision during the day. If nothing else, Dad's deteriorating physical condition curtailed his adventurous wanderings but brought new health problems. He complained of chest pains and seemed to be very short of breath. I took him in to see a cardiologist, and he told us that Dad had developed congestive heart failure. So three more medications were added to Dad's daily dual doses of psychosis medication. The cardiologist told me that the medications he was prescribing for Dad would slow him up more than he already was and suggested that I contact Dad's psychiatrist to ask if we could take him off of his two psychosis medications. I was hopeful for that and made an appointment with Dad's psychiatrist to discuss the possibility.

"Well, it won't hurt to try, but I can tell you right now it won't work," the psychiatrist commented.

"I would really like to try. Could we try for three days and see what happens?" I probed the doctor further.

"If you can watch him twenty-four seven, it won't hurt to try, but it will be futile. Your dad needs those medications," his psychiatrist cautioned me.

That was all I needed to hear—"It won't hurt to try." I wanted more than anything to get Dad off the psychosis medications, and I felt I owed it to him to try. I immediately called Connie and told her of my intention.

"Garry, you don't know what it is like to live with Dad when he is not on his medication," she said, trying to dissuade me. "I had to do it for six months, and it was pure torture! I am telling you not to try it. So when you find out for yourself, don't say I didn't try to warn you."

"I have to try. I would want him to try it for me if it were the other way around," I elucidated.

That Friday night I gave Dad his heart medications but withheld his haloperidol and lithium. I had taken Monday off so I had three days to watch him constantly while I ran the experiment. Saturday morning, I awoke to a very anxious and agitated father. He seemed extremely on edge and suspicious of what was going on around him. Paranoia was just the start. I had prepared myself for a rough first day, so I babysat him, trying to keep him calm and reassure him that everything was OK. That afternoon I was taking a break from him when I heard him holler for me to come to his room. I found Dad laughing hysterically, looking and pointing out the window.

"Look at that," Dad said with a laugh.

I looked out and saw nothing amiss. I asked, "What is it that you want me to see, Dad?"

"In the tree! There are naked men climbing in that tree and running in our yard," Dad reported through his laughter.

There were, of course, no men in the tree, let alone naked ones, but I laughed and let it be with no argument to the contrary. Later that afternoon I was summoned to his room again; this time it was to see the lions and bears in our yard. Dad was pointing to our large decorative rocks in our yard, convinced they were alive.

OK, it wasn't off to a good start, but maybe the next day would be different. Evening came, and I put a very hyper Dad to bed—at least he seemed to have more energy, even if it was of a negative nature. A very unhappy Mary (she, like Connie, was not in agreement with my decision to take Dad off his medication) and I both retired to our bedroom and quickly fell fast asleep.

We had not been asleep long when we were abruptly awoken by loud noises emanating from outside our house

Mary and I both shot straight up in our bed. What was that racket in the middle of the night? As soon as the sleep left our heads, we realized it was our garage doors opening and closing. I jumped out of bed and ran to the garage to find Dad standing by the wall remote controls, raising and lowering the doors. As one came down, he would raise the other one up. I put him back to bed only to be awakened again a short time later; this time is was by a loud ruckus coming from our kitchen. Mary was not happy when she went to bed and was extremely unhappy with me at this point. She was not in favor of my noble experiment with my dad and had warned me not to try it. She was clearly in Connie's camp on this! I once again got out of bed and went into the kitchen, where I discovered Dad, visibly upset, sitting at our kitchen island and glaring at the cabinets. He had every single cabinet door opened.

"Whose idea was it to put doors on the cabinets anyway?" he asked me with an underlying tone of anger. "You can't see what's in them!"

"Oh, I don't know, Dad, but I like the doors. That's the whole idea of them: I don't want to see what is in my cabinets." I slammed each door shut, allowing my frustration to get the best of me.

I put Dad back to bed and instructed him not to get up again until morning. I returned to our bed to try to salvage what was left of the night.

I was startled awake for the third time, this time by a woman's piercing scream in our bedroom. It was Mary who was screaming! Dad had entered our bedroom and was hovering over Mary's side of our bed, waiting for us to wake up. She woke up all right, and saw the shadowy figure of a man standing over her, and her subsequent earth-piercing scream was enough to wake the dead. And I awoke immediately! If Mary had been unhappy with me before, she was now livid. This time when I got up, I made Dad breakfast so that I could give him his psychosis medications. My noble experiment was a dismal failure, and I promised Connie, Mary, and myself that I would never, ever try it again.

Chapter 28

UNDER INVESTIGATION

Dad was always good about taking his medication and never objected, taking whatever was placed in front of him without question. Even when he was living by himself in North Bend, he took his medicine faithfully. Connie would place it in his pill minder each week, making it easy for him to take. I continued to fill his daily pill minder each week, keeping it on the kitchen counter where it would be in plain sight so I would not forget to give them to him each night after dinner. This system worked fine, and there never seemed to be a problem. One Friday night after retrieving and refilling the pill minder with the daily regimen of five pills—three for the heart and two for the head, for a total of thirty-five pills for the week—I began making dinner. Dad sat at the kitchen island watching me, as he occasionally would. I left to go get something and when I returned, I was surprised to see the pill minder up on the counter in front of Dad.

"Oh, you decided to take your pills early," I said as I reached for the pill minder to put it back where I kept it. Something didn't feel right when I picked it up, so I looked down at it. The pill minder that I had just filled with Dad's medication for the week was completely empty!

"Dad, what did you do with your medication?" I asked, perplexed.

Dad looked sheepishly at me, smiled, and then with a look of satisfaction on his face said, "I took them!"

"All of them?" I exclaimed. I found it hard to believe that he would take all thirty-five pills at once.

"Yeah," he said as if it was no big deal, smiling as if he had just accomplished some great feat.

"We've got to go now," I commanded him, wondering if he would remain conscious long enough for me to get him to the ER.

I got him in the car, and off we raced to the hospital. Dad seemed perfectly OK, at least for him, when we arrived at the ER, and they took us in immediately upon hearing what he had just done. The ER doctor arrived shortly and checked Dad's vitals, which appeared relatively normal. He then ordered a thick activated-charcoal concoction that is used to bind the drugs together and prevent their absorption in the stomach and intestinal tract.

"Mr. Olson, you need to drink this. I know it isn't pleasant tasting, but you need to drink it all," the doctor instructed Dad. The doctor turned to question me some more about how it happened, and Dad put the drink to his lips. He did not stop chugging until it was all gone. The doctor turned back to see Dad finishing off the last drop.

The doctor's face quickly showed his amazement. "I have never seen anyone drink that stuff like that before. That stuff is disgusting," the doctor said in disbelief.

"If you tell Dad to do something, he will do it," I told the doctor.

They wanted to hold Dad longer for observation, so we waited in the ER for about six hours. And then they decided to hold him overnight, so we had to wait even longer while they made arrangements to secure him a room.

When the doctor came in to tell us they had a room ready for us, Dad asked him, "When can a guy get something to eat around here?

"You *have* been in here for over six hours," the doctor replied. "Are you hungry?"

"No, just a habit," Dad said. The doctor smiled, clearly appreciating Dad's quick wit.

Yes, Dad did seem to have a quick wit about him these days, and this is the one thing I enjoyed about Dad since he got ill. But his newfound sense of humor did not begin to offset his mental and physical decline.

About a week after that incident, I got a call from Adult Protective Services (APS). We made an appointment for them to come to the house to talk to Dad and me. A no-nonsense gentleman from APS arrived, and he told me that the hospital had alerted them that Dad had been brought in for a drug overdose treatment. He said they needed to investigate the circumstances of Dad's "poisoning" to determine whether this was a case of elder neglect or abuse, and he told me that one or both could be considered a felony.

"The care you provide or don't provide your father makes you accountable to the state of Oregon, Mr. Olson," the man informed me.

"Well, I am glad that the state is looking out for the welfare of the elderly, as elder abuse is a serious problem," I began in all sincerity. "But I am held to a higher authority than the state when it comes to the care of my dad."

"What authority would that be?" the man snapped back at me.

"Well, first off, there would be my sister, and higher up than her would be God. It is He to whom I am ultimately accountable for the care of my dad. The state would be a distant third," I stated, letting him know where the true judgment of my care of Dad would rest.

"I am here for the state, and that is all I care about," the man said as he glared disapprovingly at me for daring to make such comments that he apparently took as an attempt to undermine *his* authority.

He went on to ask how I would be so careless as to put pills where Dad could get them.

"Well, until Dad moved in with me, he administered all his medication to himself without any problems, and for the last four years that he has lived with me, I kept them out so I would not forget to give them to him as I desire to provide the best care for my dad that I can," I explained somberly. "In the last fourteen years there has never been any problem, nor did I have any reason to believe there would be one. But ever since he gave himself an overdose, I have kept them up on this shelf where he cannot reach them, nor is he even aware of where they are." I opened the cupboard to show where I kept them, out of reach and sight of Dad.

The man asked a few more questions that I found accusatory in nature, jotting notes down as I provided answers to all of them. Finally, he informed me that he would like to talk with Dad—in private. I invited him into Dad's room and closed the door behind me as I left them to be alone.

Great, I thought. *My fate is in the hands of an insane man!*

Apparently, Dad gave the gentleman the correct answers as I was not arrested or interviewed by APS again.

Dad continued on his downhill slide, both physically and mentally, at a precipitous and ever-increasing rate. He lost control of his bladder, and often his bowels, and I bought Depends for him on a regular basis. I told Mary that I would not mind buying feminine hygiene products for her as the clerks would think it was nice of me to pick those products up for my wife and I would be considered a hero. But I hated to buy men's Depends for Dad for fear that people would think I was using them! Often, I would lead him into the shower with his clothes on and undress him in there with the water running since he had soiled himself so badly. It was a most unpleasant task, but I had committed to my brother and sister to provide care for our dad as long as I could. He was rapidly declining in his syntax and cognitive abilities. He would at this time use only one or two words to communicate, and on a good day he might put three words together, but even that seemingly simple task was becoming increasingly rare. Many days he would not or could not use any words at all. I remember that one day he came out to the living room where Mary was busy studying trying to finish her degree, and I was watching a game on TV.

"What do you need, Dad?" I asked.

"Arragh, arragh," he vocalized unintelligibly.

"Are you hungry?" I quizzed him, trying to decipher what he might need.

"Arragh," Dad uttered, shaking his head back and forth in a negative response.

"Would you like something to drink? Water? Milk?" I asked. Dad loved his milk.

"Arragh," Dad answered, shaking his head in frustration.

I got up and approached him, and I asked if he needed to be changed, to which he violently shook his head.

"Point to what you want, Dad, and I will get it for you," I encouraged him. He just shook his head slowly in frustration and then turned and walked dejectedly back to his room.

It was very painful to see my dad so physically and mentally impaired. And I knew that, as hard as it was for me, it was even more difficult and painful for him.

Chapter 29

WON'T HURT!

The wearisome winter, with its darkness and dreariness, had slowly given way to the spring season with its promise of rebirth and renewal. And it was on the Monday night of the week of Memorial Day weekend when I got a call from my son, Darek. After exchanging greetings, Darek got straight to the nature of his call.

"Dad, the reason I am calling you is to tell you that I received a message from God, and He told me that I am to share it with you," he began.

Darek is an extremely spiritually gifted young man, and where he got his gifting, I have no idea. I certainly haven't been so gifted; it could have only come from God and been of His choosing.

Darek had once shared with me that while he was attending a weekend Christian conference on faith healing, he had noticed a man about my age who was obviously in a great deal of pain and physically impaired because of it.

"Dad, it was all the man could do to navigate the stairs to the grandstand where we sat," Darek began.

Both Friday night and Saturday, Darek and the man sat in the same location, with the man sitting higher and behind him. That Saturday afternoon, there was an altar call for all who needed healing to come forward to receive prayer and healing. The man went down to where Darek was seated and told him that the Lord had told him that he was to come to him to receive his healing.

"I turned to the man to tell him that he should go on down to the front, as there were several prominent men of faith who had the gift of healing. But as I turned to tell him this, I saw the vision of a sword in his stomach, and the Lord spoke to me very clearly, saying that I was to remove the sword. I knew it was spiritual, but it was so visually vivid, and the Lord's instruction was unmistakable. So I told the man that I was being shown that there was a sword protruding from his stomach and the Lord said I was to remove it."

"I know," said the man. "I have stomach cancer."

"I reached for the sword to remove it, but when I touched it, I pulled back my hand immediately. I knew it was a spiritual sword so I did not expect to feel anything when I grabbed it. But I could feel the cold hard metal of the handle, and it startled me. I wasn't expecting that! I regained my composure and once again took hold of the handle. It took every ounce of my strength to remove the sword. And finally, when I was able to pull it out, I saw a gooey, blackish glob on the end of it. I then described to the man what I was seeing."

"It is the cancer," he told me. "I felt it leave me when you pulled the sword out!"

Darek told me that the man had no trouble with the stairs after that, even walking about a mile to buy lunch at a nearby Subway the next day. Darek and the man kept in touch via email after this fateful meeting and became good friends. The man shared with Darek that his doctor was amazed when he went in for his checkup and told him the cancer was gone. But the doctor was unbelieving when the man told him what had taken place and why it was gone.

Several years later, Darek got a phone call from the man saying that he had been diagnosed with a severe heart condition and the Lord had told him that there would be no healing this time, as his time had come. He asked Darek if he would speak at his funeral, where he could meet and share the story of his miraculous cure from cancer with his family and friends. When the man passed, Darek attended his funeral to speak and shared the story with the man's friends and family as he had been asked.

This story and others like it that Darek had shared with me in the past caused me to take special notice when he announced that night on the phone that he had received a message from God and that he was to share it with his dad.

"Dad, God told me that not only is He going to heal Grandpa, but he will be saved also!"

"Wow! Praise God, son," I said. At least that is what my outside voice said. My inner voice, however, was saying, *Darek, you have no idea what you just said. You haven't seen your grandpa for several months now, and you don't know how severely ill Dad is. And besides that, he is an avowed atheist, denying the very existence of God his entire life! How is it to be that Dad as an old, insane man accepts Jesus as his Lord and Savior? How can this even be possible? Let alone be somehow miraculously cured from this insanity that has a firm grip on his soul? I know all things are possible with God, but why would He choose to bless Dad, of all people?*

Darek then informed me that he was going down to Coos Bay to spend Memorial Day weekend with some of his high school friends. He said that he was coming down Wednesday night on his way to Coos Bay and that he wanted to stop off for a quick visit and pray for his grandpa.

"Well, let's hope that Dad will let you," I replied. I couldn't imagine that Dad—the man who had scolded

Larry by stating, "There is no God"—would allow someone to pray over him.

The following Wednesday night, Darek stopped by as he said he would. Dad was lying on his couch as usual when Darek arrived. When he saw his grandson enter, Dad's face lit up, and he sat up on the couch to greet him. Dad had always thought highly of his grandson and was delighted to see him.

"Hi, Darek," Dad said. I was glad that Dad was having a good day and could at least communicate with Darek, even if it was of a limited "two-word" nature.

Darek walked straight into his grandpa's room and stood in front of him as he sat on the couch.

"Can I pray for you, Grandpa?" Darek asked.

I held my breath as my dad looked up at his grandson.

"Won't hurt," Dad replied with another two-word response.

Darek placed his hands on his grandfather's head, and amazingly Dad bowed his head. Darek prayed for him. He then visited with us briefly and said goodbye as he left for his journey down to Coos Bay.

Several years later when we were talking about that phone call, Darek shared that, when he had first heard from God what God was going to do and then he also instructed to tell me what he was told, he said he actually began to reason with God.

"Dad, the voice I heard came out of nowhere. I wasn't even thinking about Grandpa. But when I heard God speaking, it was a plain as you and I are talking right now. When God said I was to tell you what He had told me, I began questioning Him. I told Him that He could heal and save Grandpa without me having to tell my dad! 'If I tell Dad, he will think I am losing it,' I contended.

"You do what I tell you to do, and I will do what I say I AM going to do," the Lord chastened me.

"So I knew I had to call and tell you. But I was afraid you would think that I am going out of my mind myself."

"Well, to tell you the truth son, the thought did cross my mind," as I confessed my lack of faith.

Chapter 30

I WAS QUITE THE CHARACTER, WASN'T I?

On Friday night of the same week of Darek's call and visit, I went to fill Dad's pill minder, as was my custom, for the upcoming week. I grabbed the now empty pill minder and the five vials of medicine from the cupboard. Something didn't feel right when I grabbed the vials of medicine, and it wasn't! Two of the vials were empty! How could this be? If, after filling Dad's pills for the week, I didn't have at least seven pills left in a vial, I do not place it back in the cupboard. I always put those on the counter so that I would have at least one week to get them refilled. This was my job! This was what I did for my dad! I had not failed him once in the last five years that he had been living with me. Yet here I was with two empty vials, not even a single pill left in either of them to put in his pill minder for the following week. I stared at the bottom of the two empty vials in disbelief! How could this possibly have happened? Nothing like this had ever happened in more than two hundred times I had repeated this practice. Thinking back to the previous week, I began to vaguely remember that, yes, after filling the pill minder the previous Friday evening, I did have two empty vials, and I distinctly remembered setting them on the counter as a reminder to get them refilled. How on earth did they get back in the cupboard? I quickly looked at the clock; it was getting late in the afternoon. Would I have time to make it to the pharmacy to get the needed medicine? The clock read 6:04! My heart sank. The pharmacy closed at 6:00 p.m., and it was Friday night. Dad needed his medications that night, and the pharmacy would be closed Saturday and Sunday. *Oh, no!* I thought. *This is Memorial Day weekend; they will be closed Monday also! It will be Tuesday of next week at the earliest before I can get Dad the medicine he so desperately needs.*

My heart was heavy. I was distraught and deeply disappointed with myself, for I had failed my dad, not to mention my sister and my wife. I held the two empty vials so that I could see what medications Dad would have to do without for the next three days. The first empty vial read "haloperidol." The second one read "lithium." Dad's two psychosis medications!

Why, God, did it have to be these two? It would be three long days and nights of pure torture. We had traveled down this road before, and it had been a rocky one indeed!

One might surmise that I would immediately think, "*This is of God. He knows that I would never take Dad off this medication.*" But alas, I confess that the thought never crossed my mind. I was only thinking how this was going to impact me.

I had promised Mary and Connie that I would never take Dad off these medications again, so God took charge as He always does and set His plan in motion. Darek's revelation didn't occur to me that evening. I was too concerned that my wife was going to "kill" me! My concern at that time was only for myself. How was I going to survive a three-day weekend with Dad off his medication and keep him and my failure from Mary?

Oh, pitiful man that I am, how long must Jesus suffer with me for *my* lack of faith?

I gave Dad his heart medications, and he never even asked about the other two, nor would I expect him to. His mind was too far gone for him to realize that I had given him three pills instead of the usual five. And I certainly wasn't going to tell my wife of my horrendous mistake. No sense in facing her wrath until I had to. You know how we husbands are: Don't let the wife know that you blew it until you have to! We ate our dinner, with Mary and Dad unaware of my mistake and me sick to my stomach. I hoped that Dad would have a restful night; heaven knows I was going to need a good night's sleep for the long three-day weekend that was to come.

The night was a peaceful one, and I was thankful for that. I got up early, well before Mary, and went quickly into Dad's room to check on him. Mary would be studying that weekend, cramming for her finals as she was almost done with her schooling to complete her degree. How could I possibly keep Dad separated from her with him off his psychosis medication? Surely it had left his system by then and the nightmare would soon commence. When I reached Dad's room, I asked him how he was doing.

"Fine, son," was his two-word reply.

Well, at least he could say two words today, which was always a good sign.

"Are you feeling anxious at all?" I probed.

Dad did not verbalize an answer; he just shook his head no as he looked up at me curiously.

I made everyone breakfast when Mary got up; I was going to need all the points from her I could get. After breakfast she cracked open her books. Even with her working full-time and going to school as well, she was on track to graduate summa cum laude, and she was committed to that goal in addition to the completion of her bachelor's studies.

I had to figure out a way to keep Dad separated from her. I cleaned up from breakfast and checked on Dad, who seemed to still be under the influence of his psychosis medications as he was calm and not agitated or anxious. I was building a gazebo on the back of our property and went outside to resume working on it. I would go into the house every hour or so to check on Dad and make sure he wasn't starting to disrupt and irritate Mary with his antics, which were sure to come.

"How are you doing, Dad?" I asked him for about the fourth time that morning.

"Doing fine, son," Dad replied, giving me a puzzled look.

Wow, I thought in amazement. *Dad just said a three-word sentence.* I couldn't remember the last time he had done that; it certainly had been a while. I turned and headed back outside to resume my gazebo project.

So far, so good, I thought.

A short time later, I once again went in to check on Dad.

"How are you feeling, Dad? Are you feeling anxious at all?"

"Feeling fine, son. Why do you keep asking?" Dad replied, obviously feeling a little perplexed.

Feeling-fine-son-Why-do-you-keep-asking: one, two, three, four, five, six, seven, eight—eight words! It had been over a year since I had heard him put together that many words at one time coherently. Immediately I felt convicted, for it was the first time I thought about what Darek had told me about God's promise to him. I fell to my knees praising God and asking for forgiveness, for my only concern the last twenty-four hours was for myself and how I was going to keep my mistake concealed from my wife. And all the time God was fulfilling his promise.

That Saturday night was another peaceful night's sleep.

When I got up Sunday morning, I checked on Dad, who was doing excellent, and after fixing him breakfast I cleaned up and left for church. Mary stayed home with Dad, she was unaware that it had now been more than sixty hours since Dad had taken his last psychosis medications. I sat there in the church oblivious to what was taking place in my surroundings. As I later told Pastor Jim Holmes, I never listened to a word he preached that Sunday. He said it was all right, that it happens a lot! I just sat there in church that Sunday morning with my head bowed in prayer and humility, thanking God and asking for His forgiveness for my lack of faith.

Oh, Father, I believe! Help me with my unbelief!

God had made a covenant with my son.

Darek was obedient.

Dad said yes (or "won't hurt") to prayer.

And as for me, I was just like the first Adam, trying to hide my shame and failure.

Dad continued improving, and when Tuesday came, I went to the pharmacy and picked up the psychosis medications that I knew I was never to give him again. Of course, I hadn't run out of Dad's medication; it had all been part of God's plan to do what He knew I would not do! Although I continued to administer Dad's heart medication, the haloperidol and lithium remained in the cupboard, unopened and unused.

About three week later Mary was busy studying and I was on the couch next to her watching a game on TV when Dad came out of the den and stood waiting for me to acknowledge his presence.

"Hi, Dad. What can I do for you?" I asked.

"I was just wondering when a guy could get something to eat around here," he asked, smiling.

"Well, it is close to lunchtime. I will fix you something to eat and bring it to you," I replied. Dad smiled and turned around to go into his room.

Mary, deeply absorbed in her studies, had not looked up from her textbook, so I asked her, "Have you noticed how good Dad has been doing lately with his communications?"

"Yes, he does seem to be doing really well lately," she responded.

"Well, you remember what Darek had said about what he had heard from God regarding Dad being healed and saved?"

She looked up at me, and I began my confession to her for the first time, telling her how I had "run out" of Dad's medication and all that had transpired since then.

Mary stared at me in disbelief that I had not informed her of what had been taking place before then. I was getting the evil eye, and since Mary has only one eye, when she gives you the evil eye, you get the *evil eye!* But then I did break my promise to her not to take Dad off his medication ever again.

"You have bought the pills, haven't you?" she demanded of me.

"Yes, I bought his pills, but he won't need them," I responded assuredly. "Dad has been healed!"

"I am not so sure I have your faith. Keep those pills handy!" she demanded.

I just smiled at her as I got up to fix Dad something to eat. Later that day, I called Connie and asked when she planned on coming up to visit Dad and give him his monthly haircut. Dad loved getting haircuts from his daughter and visiting with her. Connie and Terry were temporarily living in Albany, less than an hour away, so she was able to visit with Dad more often. Connie said she would be up the following weekend. I had shared with her what Darek had told me, but I had yet to tell her that Dad hadn't had any psychosis medication for more than a month now.

Connie arrived, and as she was standing in our foyer just outside of Dad's room, I reminded her of what Darek had told me and informed her that Dad hadn't had any psychosis medication since Memorial Day weekend. Connie, like Mary, stared at me in disbelief.

"Are you just going to stand there talking with your brother, or are you going to come in and visit with your father?" Dad asked, growing impatient waiting for us to finish with our conversation.

"When was the last time you heard Dad put together a sentence like that?" I asked Connie, who was looking at Dad with astonishment

"Darek has a lot of faith, you have a little faith, and I don't have any faith. Keep those pills handy," Connie cautioned me as she turned to go visit with Dad.

I couldn't help but smile and give thanks as I stood there watching my sister have a normal conversation with her dad, the first in more than fifteen years!

A week later, I was out finishing my gazebo project, and Mary was in the kitchen when Dad came out and asked her where I was.

"He's outside working on the—mmm, the ..." Mary started telling Dad, but she found herself unable to think of the correct word. "Oh the, the—augh!"

"The gazebo," Dad offered.

"Yes, Dad, he is out working on the gazebo," Mary replied, chuckling in amusement at the irony of what had just transpired.

Dad had just provided a word for Mary to finish her sentence. Just a few weeks earlier it had been us providing words for him.

Every time I began telling Dad about anything that had happened since we had moved him to Oregon, he had no recollection of it. I was amazed to discover that Dad had no memory of anything that had happened in the last fifteen years while he was in his psychotic state. He shared with me that the only memory he had of that time was that of

Darek placing his hand on his head and praying for him. He remembered that! He had no memory of what had happened in in California, the two arrests and his incarceration, the move to Oregon, or even the little blue house in North Bend where he had lived for more than ten years. Nor did he remember before moving in with Mary and me. He had lived with us for almost five years, but he had no memory of any of it except for his grandson praying over him.

I shared all of Dad's acts and misadventures with him. I can only imagine what he must have been thinking as I filled in the last fifteen years for him. He did not know who the current president was and had no recollection of the 9/11 attacks or any of the other major events that had occurred during the time of his illness.

One day as I shared the story of him and the DMV lady, Dad laughed heartily and said, "I was quite the character, wasn't I?"

"Yes, Dad, you were quite the character!"

He continued improving, and it was amazing to have my dad back, sane and rational.

One day he came out of his room looking a little frustrated and upset.

"What's up, Dad?" I asked.

"Well, I haven't had an accident in a long time, and I was wondering if I still needed to wear these things? I hate them," he said, tugging at the top of his Depends.

"No, you haven't," I agreed. "Let's get you into some tighty-whiteys!" I got up and got Dad some briefs, and he never donned the dreaded Depends again.

Chapter 31

SECOND COVENANT FULFILLED

It was the middle of summer and quite warm one day when I arrived home from work. As I walked through the front door, I saw Dad in his room that was just to my left, off our foyer. He was sitting on a dining room chair and watching TV. Dad preferred our padded dining room chairs to his recliner, or even to the couch these days, and it was nice to see him sitting upright instead of horizontal all of the time. As warm as it was, Dad was wearing just a white T-shirt with his blue jeans.

"Hi, Dad," I said as I entered his room. I felt the presence of the Holy Spirit, and I was compelled to share the gospel of Jesus Christ with my dad.

"Dad, I have a question for you," I announced. Dad looked up at me from his chair. "How many fish do you think you have you taken out of the ocean? Thousands? Tens of thousands?"

"I don't know, son. It would have to be in the tens of thousands, I imagine," he answered, looking a little puzzled as to why I would be asking him such a random question.

"Well, let me ask you this: How many fish did *you* put into the ocean?"

"None," Dad responded with an even more puzzled look on his face.

"Well then, I will ask you this: If you did not put a single fish in the ocean yet took tens of thousands out of it, how many did you thank God for?"

"None," he answered somberly, staring at me intently.

"Dad, you took tens of thousands of fish out of God's ocean, providing a very good living for yourself, yet you did not thank God for even one? God loves you, Dad, giving you fish you could not provide, even though you never bothered to thank Him, not even for one of them. He even healed you, and you did not ask Him, nor thank Him. He healed you not because you are a man of faith, for you have none, denying His very existence your entire life. He did not heal you because I am a man of great faith, for my faith is weak! He healed you because of the faith and obedience of your grandson and because He *loves you!*"

"Now let me ask you this: Which one of your friends would you ask me to die for?"

"None," he replied, visibly shaken by my question.

"Well then, which one of your enemies would you send me to die for?" I demanded of him.

"None!" Dad answered even more emphatically.

"Dad, you have been an enemy of God your entire life. Yet He *loves you.*" As I shared this truth with Dad, I saw tears forming in his eyes that, in a torrent, cascaded over onto his cheeks. This man whom I had never seen cry once during my entire life with him or even so much as tear up. Not even at his mother's funeral did one tear fall onto his cheek, and oh, how he loved his mother!

"He sent his Son to die for you, Dad, even while you were still His enemy. Oh, how God must love you, Dad!"

The tears were now streaming from Dad's eyes uncontrollably. I had never seen a man—or a woman, for that matter—cry so hard. His T-shirt became soaked from his tears and clung to his chest. It became so soaked that it could no longer hold the tears that were falling upon it, and they were now literally bouncing off his heaving chest as he sobbed uncontrollably.

"Dad, do you want to ask God for His Son, Jesus, to be your Lord and Savior?"

"Yes," Dad said, still sobbing but scarcely audible and nodding as the tears were still falling from his eyes.

Kneeling next to my dad, I took his hand in mine and led him in a sinner's prayer. Dad accepted the free gift of salvation that afternoon and became a child of God. And so it was, God's fulfillment of the second covenant that He gave to my son.

Chapter 32

THE FINAL BAR CROSSING

The most miraculous of summers was coming to an end, and it was a week before the start of the Labor Day weekend. As I arrived home from work, our daughter, Ashley, who was visibly upset, greeted me in our living room.

"What's the matter, sweetheart?" I asked her.

"Grandpa told me he wanted to die," she began. "I asked him why he would want to do that, and he said because it is just too hard to live anymore!"

"That's OK, Ashley," I said trying to reassure her. "His body is tired, and he has accepted Jesus as his Savior. He has lived a long life. I am sure the day will come when living becomes too hard for me and I too will want to die, and that will be OK."

The following week I came home to find Dad sleeping, sitting in his dining room chair. He was wearing his white T-shirt, and his chest was slowly heaving with each deliberate breath.

"Dad! Why don't you move to the couch to sleep?" I hollered at him. He wasn't wearing his hearing aids, so I spoke loudly so that he would hear me. He did not stir. He could fall asleep anywhere and in the most awkward of positions, but he looked so precarious perched on that chair, his head slumped to his chest. I was afraid he would fall over and hit the floor.

"*Dad!*" I hollered, louder this time. But once again, he did not stir; it was then that I noticed that a large pool of drool was wetting his T-shirt beneath his slumped head. I moved next to him and for then second time I knelt down next to my dad, this time so that I could look up into his face. When I looked into his eyes and saw their dark, empty hollowness, I knew he was gone.

I called 9-1-1 for an ambulance and then called my sister. I told Connie that the ambulance was on its way to get Dad. "He is still breathing, Connie, but he is gone," I told her. "I looked into his eyes, and when I saw them, I knew he was gone."

Connie met me at the hospital, and when the doctor came out after examining the scans that were performed on Dad, he told us what I already knew. Our dad was gone; he was still breathing, but he had no discernable brain activity.

"Your dad has suffered a massive stroke to his brain stem, and this is the worst possible location for a stroke to occur. It virtually shuts everything off. His breathing is merely reactionary for now; it too will eventually cease, as he has no brain activity. We will make him as comfortable as possible," the doctor continued. "Although we do not believe he is in any pain or can even feel any, we will give him a morphine drip just to make sure. We will also administer oxygen to aid in his breathing."

"Why are you administering the oxygen?" I asked. "So he will breathe a few hours longer?"

"That's a good question," the doctor responded.

"I would not want oxygen given to me if I was in Dad's condition, and I know Dad would not want it either," I shared with him. The doctor nodded in agreement and withheld the additional administration of oxygen.

The next morning, I went to the hospital to see my dad. I shaved his face and talked to him as he lay motionless on the bed. It was all I could do for my dad now, and the following day I did the same. As I finished shaving him on the second day, I looked around the room and saw a sink in the corner.

"Look, Dad," I said to him. "Here is the water. What is to hinder you from being baptized?" I asked, recalling the story of the baptism of the Ethiopian eunuch in Acts 8:36-37.

I went over to the sink and cupped my hands under the running water. I filled them and returned to the bed where Dad lay.

"Dad, you have accepted Jesus as your Lord and Savior," I began. "I baptize you in the name of the Father, the Son, and the Holy Spirit!" I slowly let the water slip from my hands and trickle down onto his forehead.

On the third morning, before I left the house, I received a call from the hospital informing me that Dad had taken his last breath.

The following spring, Larry and his wife, Judy, came out from Boston to join Connie and me and our families at the jetty to the Coos Bay harbor to say goodbye to our dad. They each took turns sharing about our dad and their grandpa, and then I shared a few words. We joined together and closed with a prayer of thanksgiving to God for His redemptive work in Dad's life. For now we knew him as the loving and caring man we had always hoped for but never dreamed would be a possibility—a man named Max, whom we are proud to call Dad and Grandpa.

As we said our final goodbyes, I scattered Dad's ashes into the ocean breeze and watched as they were carried out onto his beloved Pacific Ocean for his final bar crossing. And just then, as if on cue, a king salmon leaped up out of the water as if to pay homage to the old fisherman, an intriguingly complex man who was healed and saved by God's amazing grace and love for us all.

The End
and Dad's Beginning